MW00996612

Hip-Hop and Spoken Word Therapy in School Counseling

This volume recognizes the need for culturally responsive forms of school counseling and draws on the author's first-hand experiences of working with students in urban schools in the United States to illustrate how hip-hop culture can be effectively integrated into school counseling to benefit and support students.

Detailing the theoretical development, practical implementation and empirical evaluation of a holistic approach to school counseling dubbed "Hip-Hop and Spoken Word Therapy" (HHSWT), this volume documents the experiences of the school counselor and students throughout a HHSWT pilot program in an urban high school. Chapters detail the socio-cultural roots of hip-hop and explain how hip-hop inspired practices such as writing lyrics, producing mix tapes and using traditional hip-hop cyphers can offer an effective means of transcending White, western approaches to counseling. The volume foregrounds the needs of racially diverse, marginalized youth, while also addressing the role and positioning of the school counselor in using HHSWT.

Offering deep insights into the practical and conceptual challenges and benefits of this inspiring approach, this book will be a useful resource for practitioners and scholars working at the intersections of culturally responsive and relevant forms of school counseling, spoken word therapy and hip-hop studies.

Ian Levy is assistant professor of Counseling and Therapy at Manhattan College, US.

Explorations in Mental Health

Africana Peoples in China
Psychoanalytic Perspectives on Migration Experiences, Identity, and Precarious Employment
C. Jama Adams

Perspectives on Intercultural Psychotherapy
An Igbo Group Analyst's Search for his Social Identity
Okeke Azu-Okeke

Pet Loss, Grief, and Therapeutic Interventions
Practitioners Navigating the Human-Animal Bond
Edited by Lori Kogan & Phyllis Erdman

Frantz Fanon's Psychotherapeutic Approaches to Clinical Work
Practicing Internationally with Marginalized Communities
Edited by Lou Turner and Helen A. Neville

Deinstitutionalizing Art of the Nomadic Museum
Practicing and Theorizing Critical Art Therapy with Adolescents
Eva Marxen

Applications of a Psychospiritual Model in the Helping Professions
Principles of InnerView Guidance
Cedric Speyer and John Yaphe

Effective Group Therapies for Young Adults Affected by Cancer
Using Support Groups in Clinical Settings in the United States
Sarah F. Kurker

Fostering Resilience Before, During, and After Experiences of Trauma
Insights to Inform Practice Across the Lifetime
Edited by Buuma Maisha, Stephanie Massicotte and Melanie Morin

Hip-Hop and Spoken Word Therapy in School Counseling
Developing Culturally Responsive Approaches
Ian Levy

For more information about this series, please visit www.routledge.com/ Explorations-in-Mental-Health/book-series/EXMH

Hip-Hop and Spoken Word Therapy in School Counseling

Developing Culturally Responsive Approaches

Ian Levy

With a foreword by Christopher Emdin

Routledge
Taylor & Francis Group

NEW YORK AND LONDON

First published 2021
by Routledge
605 Third Avenue, New York, NY 10158

and by Routledge
2 Park Square, Milton Park, Abingdon, Oxon, OX14 4RN

*Routledge is an imprint of the Taylor & Francis
Group, an informa business*

© 2021 Taylor & Francis

Library of Congress Cataloging-in-Publication Data
Names: Levy, Ian, author.
Title: Hip-hop and spoken word therapy in school counseling :
developing culturally responsive approaches / Ian Levy.
Description: New York, NY : Routledge, 2021. | Series: Explorations in
mental health | Includes bibliographical references and index.
Identifiers: LCCN 2020058072 (print) | LCCN 2020058073 (ebook) |
ISBN 9780367903428 (hardback) | ISBN 9781003023890 (ebook)
Subjects: LCSH: Educational counseling–United States. | Hip-hop–
United States. | Spoken word poetry–United States. | Culturally relevant
pedagogy–United States. | Music, Influence of–United States. | Music
therapy for teenagers–United States.
Classification: LCC LB1027.5 .L46 2021 (print) | LCC LB1027.5 (ebook)
| DDC 371.4/22–dc23
LC record available at https://lccn.loc.gov/2020058072
LC ebook record available at https://lccn.loc.gov/2020058073

ISBN: 978-0-367-90342-8 (hbk)
ISBN: 978-0-032-00198-2 (pbk)
ISBN: 978-1-003-02389-0 (ebk)

Typeset in Baskerville
by SPi Global, India

To my family:
Joanna, Claudia, Howard, Hikari, Paul, Elana and Susanna

Contents

Foreword

The most impactful scholarly work related to teaching, learning, counseling or any profession focused on the well-being of young people have
not been descriptions of new phenomena or the use of new technologies, but uncoverings of practices that have always existed within silenced
communities. They are approaches that have gone unnamed or unex-
plored for far too long because of the unwillingness of those who hold
power to see beyond what they have learned or enact practices that are
beyond what they have experienced or inherited. What Ian Levy has
done in this work is use himself and his experiences as a tool for illuminating what has always existed. This is accomplished through an exploration of the personal – his own experiences as a student of hip-hop and
his own narratives of his struggles and successes as a counselor within
schools that serve the most underserved. Each narrative carries the same
powerful refrain – hip-hop is therapy. Whether through powerful theoretical exploration, research study or engaging story, we are introduced
or reintroduced to this fundamental principle throughout this work.
Not only do we get reminded as often as we need to that hip-hop is
therapy, Levy reminds us that hip-hop is culture; hip-hop artists are
counselors; hip-hop youth are authors, thinkers, creators, reflectors, sto-
rytellers, dreamers and hold the answers to all the questions about what
they need to be fully actualized.

Through the story of Levy's discovery of hip-hop, we see the role that
the culture plays as not just an academic topic to be studied, but a phenomenon that has changed the life of not just the researcher/academic
but a young man in search of his own authentic self. It is through this
experiential lens that we learn with the author, and also come to understand why and how hip-hop is therapy. The simple moments where one
gets filled with inspiration that triggers a new direction of thought and
provokes introspection is the beginning of healing. The studio is akin to
the counselor's office. It is a space that signals freedom – a home away
from home or a solace in a world that denies one full humanity. When
Levy builds studios with young people, they build a home together.
They become family and the sacred space they have developed together

becomes a site for healing. Rituals are built in this place. Imagination is activated and the academic self that school oftentimes relegates to a performance becomes embodied. By this, I mean that the work of the hip-hop educator or counselor is to help young people to reimagine an academic and intellectual self that schools have told them is not them. Because hip-hop has been misidentified as a problem to be solved or an identity that it is anti-school, young people who are deeply entrenched in the culture and see/feel/experience it as the only space where they can be fully themselves are taught to believe that they are unsolved problems and are anti-school. The work that Levy outlines here and the creation of space for the healing practices that already exist in communities to be sanctioned in schools and used to reimagine young people's relationships to school allow them to dream bigger than what they have been told they are and shatter expectations that have limited their infinite potential. The entire enterprise of teaching and counseling youth who are deeply embedded in hip-hop with hip-hop is revolutionary in its elegant simplicity. It is simply calling forth who they are in the exercise of allowing them to become more than what we have fashioned them to be.

If, as Levy describes in this work, the system of education has been designed to rob hip-hop youth of their voice, then it is essential that it find ways to restore that voice if it is interested in any form of restitution for the historical wrongs it has done. Of course, the assumption that our current system of education is interested in restoration or restitution is a great one. We are led to believe that this is the case. The language in teacher and counselor education programs seems to bend toward the arc of social justice. Terms like cultural relevance, cultural responsiveness, anti-racist, abolitionist, equity focused are littered across curricula. However, in practice, the work of teachers and counselors have been about how those terms have been thought about, and not about how they are embodied. How do teachers live out relevance? How do counselors become anti-racist? What do any of these terms look like when one is in front of actual young people and not figments of our collective imagination who exist with a certain downtroddenness and brokenness and that we are supposed to save from themselves and their communities with our degrees. I suggest as Levy alludes to in this book that the work is about seeing them as whole, seeing their culture as valuable and then, most importantly, restoring to them what schools and society have robbed them of. Counseling, like good teaching, is about restoration of a sense of self that one comes into the earth with. It is allowing one to see their own genius even in a world that denies it. It is opening up doors of possibility for young people to walk through while arming them with themselves. It is the work of restitution.

One major path of restitution for Levy and in hip-hop is in the revealing of the magic of lyric writing. Holding the prose from our griots who speak over beats with inflections that are unique and create amazing feats with every move of their feet in the circle that is the cypher. The holding up of raps as complex text to be constructed and then deconstructed. To tease out the emotion and intent behind a line, and then sit in and with it until it reveals what its intention is, is revolutionary work. In the digging beneath the surface is where the magic appears – the revelation of my mental state of the author, the psychology of the community, the calls for help or even the affirmations of one's own brilliance. In lyric writing – especially in community as it happens in Levy's work is group therapy that overshadows the more academic or clinical version of it by leaps and bounds. It is sharing and exchanging ideas in a way that is equally as vulnerable and affirming in one fell swoop. Levy names part of this process as spoken word therapy. In my work, I have named parts of it as reality pedagogy. We have even worked together to name some collision of our ideas as Hip-Hop and Spoken Word Therapy. At the end of the day, it is just basic hip-hop shit. What we do is make connections between what is genius outside of school so that it can help to heal inside the school with instructions for how to do it for those who need a play by play on a path to freedom for our young people.

The secret sauce for being able to transfer the magic from outside of the school into the classroom and/or counseling space without fear of being perceived by youth as pandering or being disingenuous is authenticity. Levy uses the word realness. Hip-hop calls it Knowledge of Self. Many, in the pursuit of being seen as real or authentic spend their efforts trying to be like their students. This approach to being seen as authentic is actually the most inauthentic thing one can do. One cannot try to develop the same passions, interest, modes of speech or ways of communicating as youth and expect to be seen as anything other than an impostor. The self-work to be real is to spend time with yourself to understand who you are and what got you to where you are. When one has done that self-work, they can take up the task of creating the conditions for their students to do the same thing. Culture – like hip-hop emerges on the road to creating those conditions and authenticity recognizes itself when it is expressed in others even if it takes different forms in each individual. Teachers and counselors who know and express who they authentically are create the conditions (by their very presence) that allow young people to do the same. They model for young people that it is okay to be full and whole and that they operate without the hubris that many teachers carry that inhibits them from working WITH young people to create the environments they need to thrive. .

This working WITH is not only about democratizing every aspect of teaching, learning and counseling but also about research. It embraces Youth Participatory Action Research (YPAR) and the concept of youth as creators, thought leaders and innovators. It then connects this concept to hip-hop cyphers and names them as a non-institutional iteration of the cypher, a model for the ideal classroom and a model for the ideal type of community of practice necessary for the classroom.

This work is powerful because hip-hop is powerful. It is important because counselors and counseling is important. It is the next frontier for counseling education and education writ large because hip-hop has the answers to all that plagues our society. I am thankful because Ian Levy has been and continues to be a good steward of this work.

Dr. Christopher Emdin
November 2020

Acknowledgments

I have to thank my incredible wife, Joanna, for putting up with me for 18 months while I wrote this thing. It was a turbulent process, but you stuck by me!

Thank you to my big bro Christopher Emdin for the endless support and encouragement. You already know there is no book without your guidance, and those not-so-subtle reminders, like, "would you just write the thing, already!" – I appreciate you, always.

Special thanks to Edmund Adjapong. You are an amazing colleague, friend and research partner. I'm so grateful to share space with you. A great deal of our research is cited throughout this text and has been essential for the exploration of this model. I'm excited to continue our collaborative work!

To the rest of my #HipHopEd family Timothy Jones, Amil Cook, Courtney Rose, Ebone Emdin, Mike Dando, Gloria Ladson-Billings, Emery Petchauer, Sam Seidel, Qiana Spellman and Thandi Hicks-Harper. Your work and constant affirmation of HHSWT helped motivate me to believe in and concretize salient aspects of this model.

More thanks to Raphael Travis for helping me cultivate skills as a scholar/practitioner, and for creating a space to test the mixtape making model. Not only have you been a research partner to me, but you have been selfless in your willingness to offer junior scholars opportunities to grow and explore their work. Thank you for your mentorship, advocacy and leadership.

To two powerful forces in Hip Hop Therapy, who I have had the pleasure of working closely with. Thank you, Tomas Alvarez and John Gill, for your work with Beats, Rhymes and Life (BRL), and now our collaborative work. I see this book as part of a much larger puzzle we are working to put together.

To those in school counseling who inspire me and this work. Whether it has been an insightful conversation, collaborative research project or guest lecture, an incredible group of school counselor educators have endorsed my work. The academy can be isolating, and you each have made it feel infinitely less so. Thank you to Amy Cook, Brian Hutchison,

Kara Ieva, Matthew Lemberger-Truelove, Stuart Chen-Hayes, Cynthia Walley, Joey Estrada, Malik Henfield, George McMahon, Carol Dahir, Corine Fitzpatrick, Lisa Suzuki and Laura Owen.

To the places and people that showed me Hip-hop: Legendary Cyphers, End of The Week, Freestyle Mondays, The Bronx, La Salle and Broadway, AMS II, Baxter Wordsworth, Rabbi Darkside, BS, Manny Faces, Makil Amin, Farbeon, PhaseOne, DJ Static, Crimdella, Osyris Anthem and many more.

Introduction
An Ode to Hip-Hop

Hip-Hop as a Personal Journey

It is 2009, I am standing inside of a dorm room with four other under-graduate students, a microphone in my hand. As a soul-influenced hip-hop beat boomed through an amplifier on top of a desk, I nervously prepared to share a verse about self-doubt and not feeling supported. These are feelings I had not disclosed to others, as they are connected to my being diagnosed as dyslexic, being academically tracked to take remedial classes during my middle and high school years, and then developing low academic self-efficacy. Despite my reservation to open up about these thoughts and feelings, the rhymes spoken through the mic are met with emphatic slaps on the back, and words of encouragement. How could it be that disclosing vulnerable thoughts and feelings, for which I have felt judged for my entire life, were radically accepted and celebrated in a college dorm room? At that point, I did not know why, but I felt addicted to this level of sharing. Suddenly my nights were full of isolated writing sessions, and conquests to find or create a beat to rhyme over, in preparation to re-enter community spaces to share my thoughts and feelings.

This initial experience with hip-hop is far from unique. Using hip-hop to express feelings was, however, authentic as it reflected hip-hop's functional use as an outlet to share untold stories (Land & Stovall, 2009). Hip-Hop originated in the 1970s South Bronx as a means for community members to discuss thoughts and feelings and offer a counternarrative regarding the beauty that was the Bronx (Chang, 2005). In hip-hop culture, it is theorized that there is an expectation that cultural participants use their art as a platform to comment on social issues, as well as their own circumstances, beliefs and worldviews (Forman, 2002; Hill, 2009). Hip-hop cultural spaces, like cyphers or open mic nights, are safe and supportive community-based platforms where participants can share rhymes and explore difficult thoughts and feelings without the fear of feeling vulnerable or week (Levy & Keum, 2014). Cyphers, much like the space I shared with my college friends, are described as codified yet unstructured spaces where individuals who identify with hip-hop culture stand in a circle and exchange information in the form of raps or dance (Levy, Emdin, & Adjapong, 2018).

After these initial dorm-room events, attending local New York hip-hop cyphers became a ritual. It was the only place I felt I could be myself. While pursuing a master's degree in counseling, I recall living a life as a student and rapper in New York City. During the day I attended lectures on group dynamics, discussing the importance of establishing group norms that help group members to build cohesion and, in so many words, submit to the process of sharing vulnerabilities within each other (Yalom & Leszcz, 2005). At night I stood in circles of rappers waiting to talk about my goals, fears, accomplishments and mistakes while being careful not to disrupt the flow of the cypher (i.e., entering too early and cutting anyone else off). The natural connection between the group-based community outlets for catharsis that hip-hop offered, and what counseling professionals desired to create in their practical group work became increasingly clear. Hip-hop appeared to organically offer participants an environment necessary for emotional disclosure to occur, the type of environment counselors dedicate their careers to establishing.

As part of that preparation to enter cyphers, I kept many iterations of a lyric journal. Inside said journal were both rhymes that came to my mind throughout daily life, as well as the writings of specific songs to process different emotional experiences. Each song chronicled a different life event, my reality. As a regular practice, a good friend of mine offered thoughts or edits on each song. Specifically, this friend asked me to clarify certain lines that he felt were not descriptive enough. The individual discussion I had with this friend about a specific rhyme, eventually led to the reconstruction of select lyrics to more accurately and vividly speak to the emotional experience at hand. While I am explaining this process in a somewhat formulaic matter, in actuality, it unfolded naturally.

Here too, however, was a connection between an organic hip-hop practice and a desirable counseling process. In our work as helpers, whether a school counselor is pulling from core humanistic principles (Rogers, 1957) or cognitive-behavioral techniques (Beck, 1963), the goal is to help a student process a presenting concern. The therapeutic relationship is evidenced as a prominent factor in supporting the healing process (Nienhuis et al. 2018), particularly when relationships can allow students can present themselves authentically and have their thoughts and feelings validated (McCarthy et al., 2019). Certain tools that a more cognitive-behavior-oriented school counselor might consider include Beck's (1963) homework assignments wherein clients document their thoughts, feelings and behaviors surrounding a presenting concern, inside a journal that they bring with them to session.

The counselor and client then discuss what is present within that journal and work toward clarifying, refining and restructuring thoughts to help produce alternate behaviors.

I continue to be struck by how closely clinical guidelines, such as the aforementioned, resemble fundamental aspects of the lyric writing process and hip-hop cultural practices. In many ways, this personal journey and relationship with hip-hop feed my scholarship and larger research agenda. In 2011, I took a graduate class on theories of counseling, where I began making many of these connections between my personal journey with hip-hop and traditional counseling processes. As a culminating assignment for this school counseling course, I wrote a theoretical paper about the use of hip-hop interventions in school counseling practice. The response from my professor and class was overwhelming, with their support leading to the paper being published in the *Journal of Poetry Therapy*. The article, Hip-Hop and Spoken Word Therapy with Urban Youth (Levy, 2012), became the impetus for subsequent work developing a model, hence writing this text. Ultimately, the validation that I had missed in my middle and high school years was discovered in and around dorm-room hip-hop cyphers and resulted in the publication of a peer-reviewed journal article on the use of hip-hop as therapy. In short, I fell in love with hip-hop culture because the community welcomed me in for the whole of who I was, celebrated my vulnerabilities and complexities with me and encouraged me to explore my potential to pursue self-actualization. Proudly, I attribute the entirety of my personal development and research interests to hip-hop culture.

Hip-Hop and Education

In fact, experiential knowledge regarding the power and potential of hip-hop culture to support one's development has led a handful of scholars to advocate for its cultural complexities (Emdin, 2010; Hill, 2009) and to push back against stereotypical perceptions that portray it as solely violent and misogynistic (Rose, 2008). Noting the growth of hip-hop culture since its establishment in the 1970s (Chang, 2005), a fair number of scholars have defined youth culture broadly as hip-hop culture (Adjapong, 2019; Emdin, 2010). Consequently, a groundswell of research explores how to integrate aspects of youth culture (hip-hop culture) into schooling praxis. Petchauer (2009) engaged in a review of educational research concerning hip-hop education, deducing that hip-hop-based curricular approaches, addressing a variety of academic outcomes, have been present in the literature since the early 2000s. Whether scholars used rap texts in classrooms to support Black and Latinx youth in analyzing literature (Morrell, 2004; Morrell & Duncan-Andrade, 2002), critical literacy (Hill, 2009) or other English language arts competencies (Stovall, 2006), the argument for approaches was largely the same – to address concerns regarding the lack of culturally responsive approaches to teaching and learning to support students academically (Petchauer, 2009). Across the last decade, approaches to hip-hop pedagogy have become a topic of increased interest across educational curricula (Ewing, 2014), including in English (Kelly, 2013, 2016) Science (Adjapong & Emdin, 2015; Emdin, 2010), Math (Amidon, 2013; Tillman, 2016) and to support civic engagement (Alim, 2011; Childs, 2014; Love, 2014, 2015).

Research on hip-hop-based strategies in therapy, broadly, span at least two decades, with specific foci on the fields of social work (Alvarez, 2012; Travis and Deepak, 2011; Tyson, 2002), psychiatry (Hakvoort, 2015; Sule & Inkster, 2014), psychology (Abdul-Adil, 2014; Dang et al., 2014), school counseling (Elligan, 2000; Gonzalez & Hayes, 2009; Levy et al., 2018; Washington, 2018), and music therapy (Geipel et al., 2018; Hadley & Yancy, 2012; Viega, 2016). While strategies in school counseling practice have been explored conceptually, and in small one-off studies, missing within the field of hip-hop education research is consistent empirical support of a singular comprehensive hip-hop and school counseling model.

In sum, hip-hop-based approaches to education have become more present in teacher education literature and practice (i.e., critiquing hip-hop lyrics and music videos to promote student's development of media literacy skills, literacy skill development or writing hip-hop songs to master science content). Within the field of counseling however, research is fairly limited. This is the case despite the fact that a bevy of researchers call for culturally sensitive approaches to counseling that transcend traditional, White and western, approaches to talk therapy. Further, the role of the school counselor is even less explored, as an essential provider of culturally responsive counseling and developmental services for young people.

Hip-Hop and Spoken Word Therapy

Drawing on five years of practice as a school counselor, as well as an additional three years as a counselor educator, this text brings together elements of counseling and hip-hop education to detail the theoretical development, practical implementation and empirical evaluation of a holistic approach to school counseling, dubbed Hip-hop and Spoken Word Therapy (HHSWT). This text will follow a pilot program in a South Bronx High School from 2014 to 2016, specifically exploring how the development of this program (where students wrote, recorded and performed emotionally themed hip-hop music) leads to a larger line of research that substantiates and concretizes HHSWT as a school counseling model.

The initial chapter of this text will serve the purpose of offering an ideological foundation for the use of hip-hop-based practices in urban school counseling. Chapter 2 details a pilot study which served as the initial development, implementation and evaluation of a HHSWT-based school counseling project with urban youth in New York City. Engaging in this project illuminated other areas necessary to explore, in order to substantiate HHSWT as a model. The third chapter explores the concept of authenticity in counseling research, as a necessary prerequisite to a successful therapeutic process generally, and HHSWT in particular. This chapter is positioned as a response to questions like, "What if I know nothing about hip-hop? Can I still engage in this work?". The answer is yes, as long as you can do it authentically. The purpose of this chapter is therefore to explore how a set of hip-hop cultural guidelines for being genuine can help counselors engage in essential self-work necessary to respond to lack of realness or authenticity youth of color feel in session.

After the initial pilot program, I realized the importance of the physical hip-hop studio space in which the pilot program was facilitated and engaged in numerous follow-up studies examining a process through which youth co-designed their own counseling offices as hip-hop studios. In Chapter 4, I will share that research, exploring the importance of studio construction in the HHSWT model. Chapter 5 explores how hip-hop mixtapes offer a framework for a culturally sensitive group counseling process, referred to as the Critical Cycle of Mixtape Creation, wherein students compose emotionally themed mixtapes to support them in critically analyzing, researching and reporting on issues of personal importance to them. In Chapter 6, the community-defined practice of hip-hop cyphers will be explored to glean implications for small-group counseling. Due to the limited amount of research on hip-hop cyphers, this chapter reports on data from a study where various hip-hop artists were interviewed about their participation in cyphers, which illuminate how they can be used to support a group counseling process. Chapter 7 of this book analyzes how HHSWT can support practicing school counselors in the professional development context, specifically in supporting their use of counseling skills essential in maintaining and facilitating HHSWT within a comprehensive school counseling program. This book concludes with an exploration of HHSWT as a holistic model for school counseling, containing a variety of elements detailed in each of the prior chapters.

References

Abdul-Adil, J. K. (2014). Modern rap music: Mining the melodies for mental health resources. *Journal of Youth Development, 9*(2), 149–152.

Adjapong, E. (2019). Towards a practice of emancipation in urban schools: A look at student experiences through the science genius battles program. *Journal of Ethnic and Cultural Studies, 6*(1), 15–27.

Adjapong, E. S., & Emdin, C. (2015). Rethinking pedagogy in urban spaces: Implementing hip-hop pedagogy in the urban science classroom. *Journal of Urban Learning, Teaching, and Research, 11*, 66–77.

Alim, H. S. (2011). Global ill-literacies: Hip hop cultures, youth identities, and the politics of literacy. *Review of Research in Education, 35*(1), 120-146. DOI: 10.3102/0091732X10383208

Alvarez, T. (2012). Beats, rhymes and life: Rap therapy in an urban setting. In S. Hadley & G. Yancey (Eds.), *Therapeutic uses of rap and hip-hop* (pp. 99–114). New York, NY: Routledge/Taylor & Francis Group.

Amidon, J. (2013). Teaching mathematics as agape: Responding to oppression with unconditional love. *Journal of Urban Mathematics Education, 6*(1), 19–27.

Armstrong, S. N., & Ricard, R. J. (2016). Integrating rap music into counseling with adolescents in a disciplinary alternative education program. *Journal of Creativity in Mental Health, 11*(3–4), 423–435.

Beck, A. T. (1963). Thinking and depression: I. Idiosyncratic content and cognitive distortions. *Archives of General Psychiatry, 9*(4), 324–333.

Chang, J. (2005). *Can't stop won't stop: A history of the hip-hop generation.* St Martin's Press.

Childs, D. J. (2014). "Let's talk about race": Exploring racial stereotypes using popular culture in social studies classrooms. *The Social Studies, 105*(6), 291–300.

Dang, S., Vigon, D., & Abdul-Adil, J. (2014). Exploring the healing powers of hip-hop: Increasing therapeutic efficacy, utilizing the hip-hop culture as an alternative platform for expression, connection. In *See you at the crossroads: Hip hop scholarship at the intersections* (pp. 169–180). Brill Sense.

Elligan, D. (2000). Rap therapy: A culturally sensitive approach to psychotherapy with young African American men. *Journal of African American Men*, 27–36.

Emdin, C. (2010). Affiliation and alienation: Hip-hop, rap, and urban science education. *Journal of Curriculum Studies, 42*(1), 1–25. doi:10.1080/00220270903161118

Ewing, E. L. (2014). Schooling Hip-Hop: Expanding Hip-Hop Based Education Across the Curriculum. *Harvard Educational Review, 84*(1), 125–128.

Forman, M. (2002). *The 'hood comes first: Race, space, and place in rap and hip-hop.* CT: Wesleyan.

Geipel, J., Koenig, J., Hillecke, T. K., Resch, F., & Kaess, M. (2018). Music-based interventions to reduce internalizing symptoms in children and adolescents: A meta-analysis. *Journal of Affective Disorders, 225*, 647–656.

Gonzalez, T., & Hayes, B. G. (2009). Rap music in school counseling based on Don Elligan's rap therapy. *Journal of Creativity in Mental Health, 4*(2), 161–172. doi:10.1080/15401380902945293

Hadley, S., & Yancy, G. (Eds.). (2012). *Therapeutic uses of rap and hip-hop.* Routledge.

Hakvoort, L. (2015). Rap music therapy in forensic psychiatry: Emphasis on the musical approach to rap. *Music Therapy Perspectives, 33*(2), 184–192.

Hill, M. L. (2009). *Beats, rhymes, and classroom life: Hip-hop pedagogy and the politics of identity.* Teachers College Press.

Kelly, L. L. (2013). Hip-hop literature: The politics, poetics, and power of hip-hop in the English classroom. *English Journal*, 51–56.

Kelly, L. L. (2016). "You don't have to claim her" reconstructing black femininity through critical hip-hop literacy. *Journal of Adolescent & Adult Literacy, 59*(5), 529–538.

Land, R. R., & Stovall, D. O. (2009). Hip hop and social justice education: A brief introduction. *Equity & Excellence in Education, 42*(1), 1–5.

Levy, I. (2012). Hip hop and spoken word therapy with urban youth. *Journal of Poetry Therapy, 25*(4), 219–224.

Levy, I., Emdin, C., & Adjapong, E. S. (2018). Hip-Hop Cypher in Group Work. *Social Work with Groups, 41*(1–2), 103–110. doi:10.1080/01609513.2016.1275265

Levy, I., & Keum, B. T. (2014). Hip-hop emotional exploration in men. *Journal of Poetry Therapy, 27*(4), 217–223. doi:10.1080/08893675.2014.949528

Love, B. L. (2014). Urban storytelling: How storyboarding, moviemaking, and hip-hop-based education can promote students' critical voice. *English Journal*, 53–58.

Love, B. L. (2015). *Imagining mattering: Hip-hop civics ed*, Intersectionality & Black Joy.

McCarthy, K. S., Zilcha-Mano, S., & Barber, J. P. (2019). Process research in psychodynamic psychotherapy: Interventions and the therapeutic relationship. In *Contemporary psychodynamic psychotherapy* (pp. 75–88). Academic Press.

Morrell, E. (2004). *Linking literacy and popular culture: Finding connections for lifelong learning*. Christopher-Gordon Publishers.

Morrell, E., & Duncan-Andrade, J. M. (2002). Promoting academic literacy with urban youth through engaging hip-hop culture. *English Journal*, 88–92.

Nienhuis, J. B., Owen, J., Valentine, J. C., Winkeljohn Black, S., Halford, T. C., Parazak, S. E., Budge, S., & Hilsenroth, M. (2018). Therapeutic alliance, empathy, and genuineness in individual adult psychotherapy: A meta-analytic review. *Psychotherapy Research, 28*(4), 593–605.

Petchauer, E. (2009). Framing and reviewing hip-hop educational research. *Review of Educational Research, 79*(2), 946–978.

Rogers, C. R. (1957). The necessary and sufficient conditions of therapeutic personality change. *Journal of Consulting Psychology, 21*(2), 95.

Rose, T. (2008). *The hip hop wars: What we talk about when we talk about hip hop–and why it matters*. Civitas Books.

Sule, A., & Inkster, B. (2014). A hip-hop state of mind. *The Lancet Psychiatry, 1*(7), 494–495. doi:10.1016/S2215-0366(14)00063-7

Stovall, D. (2006). We can relate: Hip-hop culture, critical pedagogy, and the secondary classroom. *Urban Education, 41*(6), 585–602.

Tillman, D. A. (2016). Learning from the college dropout: Depictions of numeracy and mathematics within hip-hop music. *Journal of Mathematical Education, 9*, 53–71.

Travis, R., Jr., & Deepak, A. (2011). Empowerment in context: Lessons from hip-hop culture for social work practice. *Journal of Ethnic & Cultural Diversity in Social Work, 20*(3), 203–222. doi:10.1080/15313204.2011.594993

Tyson, E. H. (2002). Hip hop therapy: An exploratory study of a rap music intervention with at-risk and delinquent youth. *Journal of Poetry Therapy, 14*(3), 131–144. DOI: 10.1023/A:1019795911358

Viega, M. (2016). Exploring the discourse in hip hop and implications for music therapy practice. *Music Therapy Perspectives, 34*(2), 138–146.

Washington, A. R. (2018). Integrating hip-hop culture and rap music into social justice counseling with black males. *Journal of Counseling & Development, 96*(1), 97–105. doi:10.1002/jcad.12181

Yalom, I. D., & Leszcz, M. (2005). *Theory and practice of group psychotherapy.* Taylor & Francis US.

1 Hip-Hop Culture, Educational History and Humanism in Relation to School Counseling

Hip-Hop Culture

In the 1970s the South Bronx underwent significant systemic and structural changes (Caro, 1974), stripping schools of their instrumental music programs (Chang, 2005). In response, local Bronx leaders promoted pro-Black messages to mobilize the community against various inequalities (Decker, 1993). Within these organized community spaces, hip-hop culture emerged. Emcees (rappers), DJs, bboys/bgirls (dancers) and Graffiti artists became primary voices creating and commenting on social issues their community (Forman, 2002). Since the beginnings of hip-hop culture, there has been a strong focus on presenting art that is a genuine reflection of who the artist is and what they have been through (Wang, 2012). Lyric writing and performing in hip-hop "connects the histories of the marginalized, echoes their pain, and concurrently articulates the stance of new people who either have been, or are being, marginalized in different spaces around the globe" (Emdin, 2010, p. 5). In this sense, Hip-hop emerged out of an urge to speak back against social conditions which oppressed mostly Black and Brown urban communities (Chang, 2005), making it an expectation that participants in the culture use their art as a platform to comment on social issues, circumstances, or particular urban beliefs and worldviews (Hill, 2009; Forman, 2002). Hip-hop as a culture has impacted and empowered youth populations across the globe, especially youth of marginalized groups, since its conception (Adjapong & Emdin, 2015; Dunley, 2000).

While the creation of hip-hop culture was part of an authentic and community-driven movement, public perception of hip-hop culture became skewed over time (Rose, 2008). Hip-hop artists have reported feeling the need to produce musical content that highlighted violence, drug use, partying and other stereotypical aspects of Black and Brown communities to access record deals (Rose, 2008). Images and music videos promoted by record labels (Reyna et al. 2009), or road shows featuring bboys and bgirls, further painted Black and Brown communities as inferior (Rose, 2008; Yousman, 2003). The deliberate stereotypical promotions of hip-hop culture ensured that mainstream demonstrations of hip-hop were no longer rooted in cultural origins (Graham, 2017). In fact, many have feared that the commercialization of hip-hop culture threatens the erasure of its cultural creativity and complexity (Thompson, 2016). The erasure of the cultural complexities of hip-hop is particularly problematic given the understanding that hip-hop culture is youth culture (Adjapong & Emdin, 2015).

Hip-Hop Culture, Assimilation and Schooling

The erasure of a group's history and cultural origins has been explored extensively by scholars, and in many cases has been tied to educational practices that oppress Black, Indigenous and other People of Color (BIPOC). Ladson-Billings (2006) elucidates historic forms of racism and xenophobia at play in the United States that, in the context of schooling, constitute part of an educational debt that cannot be overlooked as educators work toward equitable schooling systems. For example, synthesizing the work of educational historians (Anderson, 2002; Fultz, 1995; Tyack, 2004), Ladson-Billings (2006) reminds us that disparaging and racist beliefs of Black youth prevented access to university secondary schooling until 1968 after a history of being: barred from (western) education entirely during slavery, offered education post-emancipation that aimed to produce workers for the servant class and receiving schooling in incredibly difficult resource-barren environments. Ladson-Billings (2006) further details Ferg-Cadima's (2004) scholarship which identifies the historic ways in which Latinx youth have had their lived experiences denounced and been stripped of equitable access to education.

A distinct process occurred for Indigenous youth. Smith (2012) discusses how, in the late 1800s, Indigenous people's values, beliefs, voice and knowledge were lost after being colonized and imperialized by western Europeans. In her explanation of this process, Smith (2012) states that "imperialism and colonialism brought complete disorder to colonized peoples, disconnecting them from their histories, their landscapes, their languages, their social relations and their own ways of thinking, feelings and interacting with the world" (p. 29). Operating from an ideology that Indigenous people lacked intellect, imagination and the ability to create their own history, westerners erroneously believed colonial education was a mechanism to help or save Native youth from a life of savagery and forced their assimilation to dominant White and western standards of success (Smith, 2012).

Building on the work of Ladson-Billings (2006), Dr. Christopher Emdin, associate professor at Columbia University and author of *For White Folks Who Teach In the Hood: and The Rest of Y'all Too*, urged educators to "understand the oppression [Black and Brown] youth experience, the spaces they inhabit, and the ways these phenomena affect what happens in social settings like traditional classrooms" (p. 9). In public and charter schools today, Black and Brown are forced to conform to the expectations of their schools, which are often divorced from who they are, in order to be perceived/perceive themselves as successful (Emdin, 2016). It is therefore a contemporary educator's responsibility to understand the ways in which modern educational instititions enact oppressive assimilation processes that create barriers for Black and Brown youth's authentic self-expression and development, and to push back against them (Emdin, 2016). Love (2016) suggests the amalgamation of oppressive and anti-Black practices creates racist school environments that deny youth access to "inclusion, protection, safety, nurturance, and acceptance" (p. 2). The education system, largely, has piled on a historic debt, which school counselors are responsible for understanding and critiquing, given their position as professionals responsible for assisting in battling assimilatory, racist and oppressive structures that threaten BIPOC youth's development.

To navigate and survive oppressive schooling systems, Love (2016) demands the creation of educational spaces that nurture BIPOC youth's development toward a sense of wholeness. Smith (2012) suggested that "Indigenous peoples [need] to tell our own stories, write our own versions, in our own ways, for our own purposes" (p. 29), in order to "give testimony to and restore a spirit, to bring back into existence a world fragmented and dying" (p. 30). Emdin (2016) argues Black and Brown youth use hip-hop to tell their own stories, in their own ways, as a counter-narrative and vehicle through which they can reclaim their own knowledge and history. Scholars have emphasized that the hip-hop community pushes for the maintenance of authenticity as a social practice to combat the threat of assimilation (McLeod, 1999). However, both hip-hop culture and Black and Brown voices are often viewed by western culture as negative, dangerous and lacking value (Emdin, 2016). It is this very perception that has enabled traditional education systems to stand in opposition to verbal, physical and/or aesthetic displays of hip-hop, believing that by erasing hip-hop culture, education could be the vehicle through which Black and Brown youth are saved (Emdin, 2016; Love, 2019). It is because of this reality that educators and counselors have argued for the use of hip-hop practices in schools and communities since the early 1990s (Hayes, 1993; Powell, 1991; Stephens, 1992), and why scholars have called for culturally competent school counseling (Holcomb-McCoy, 2004). However, more recently hip-hop approaches to pedagogy and counseling have been anchored in culturally responsive mechanics that support youth's ability to engage in authentic self-expression despite oppressive structures that minimize their identities (Adjapong, 2019; Levy, 2019). To further explore this notion of erasing youth culture in schools, I will provide a case study that illustrates the modern enactment of these colonial processes in urban schools. Specifically, this case study explores a problematic school process I observed upon visiting an urban school. This case study is explored to offer an example of the oppression that youth experiences on a daily basis within urban schools.

A Case Study Illustrating the Erasure of Youth Culture

In 2017 I worked as a counselor educator at a University in Boston, Massachusetts. As part of this work, it was expected that I would visit multiple schools to check-in on graduate students who were completing internships as school counselors-in-training. As I stood in a line of Black and Latinx students waiting to enter a High School through a metal detector, I watched a slew of security staff stand next to the scanning system searching bags on tables – smiling as they abrasively open book-bag compartments and slung "jokes" like "I'm not going to find anything you don't want me to right?!" The high school students did not seem bothered by this, standing silently in line with headphones on waiting to be allowed into school. As someone who has an affinity for sneaker shopping, I did notice an array of Jordan sneakers on the feet of students. I had been told that as a counselor educator I needed to "dress professionally" when visiting schools, so I left my sneakers at home and sported a blazer and some Wingtips instead. It was my turn to enter the scanner. The White male security guard looked at me and happily stated, "You look like a good guy, just walk around".

Off-put, I turned the corner to the lobby of the school building where banners displaying the schools "core values" hang from the ceiling with words like "Respect", "Integrity", "Commitment" and "Honor". Varying versions of these values exist in schools across the country, and ultimately represent what it means to be an exemplary student in the school. As I walked down the hallway, I saw students switching out of their sneakers into "school shoes" (plain Black dress shoes) while being rushed to class by staff. A rule for the school, tied directly to what it means to be an exemplary student and display those core values, was to only wear black shoes. This meant that students would come to school in their own shoes and spend time switching into their school shoes before going to class. This process appeared to cause a significant hassle in the morning, even requiring the school to offer pairs of Black school shoes to students who did not have them, causing a line of students to appear outside of an office in this hallway. However, once students made this change, they were "ready" to begin their school day, as they aligned themselves with what the school deemed to be a scholar.

Connection to Oppressive Practices

For the school, in this example, one can imagine that commitment to becoming an exemplary student means arriving at school on time, wearing proper shoes and submitting to a searched entry. Note: the school appeared to respect my scholarliness instantly, a White male in a button-down and blazer. In this sense, I am both respected and perceived as an individual who displays commitment toward being scholarly based on my external appearance – dressing the part of a White male who adheres to dominant cultural norms. My being told that I "look like a good guy" confirms this and leads me to presume that the young Black and Brown youth entering this school are believed not to look like "good guys" or "girls" until they are cleared via the forced search, and put school shoes on. The physical switching of appearance under the guise of profession-alism represents the school's support of youth transitioning from bad to good, inappropriate to appropriate, disrespectful to respectful and the list goes on. Or, in colonial education terms being "released from the slavery of tribal life" (U.S. Government Printing Office, 1896, p. 18).

While the process of arriving at school in incredibly well-kept kicks represents elements of student presentation or behavior that the school demands must be removed to earn respect or demonstrate commitment, a literal opposite reality exists for students. For students, the value of arriving at school on time or "professionally dressed" pales in compari-son to the value of arriving to school looking fresh or feeling authentic. So much so that students went through the hassle of changing, just so they could wear their shoes until they enter the school building. This sounds a lot like commitment to me. Emdin (2016) discusses the impor-tance of dress and aesthetics in youth culture and being "clean". In a world where obstacles to success are vast, complex and systematically rooted, wearing a crisp pair of sneakers to feel good about yourself is often a self-esteem boosting tactic (Emdin, 2016). This cathartic commit-ment to persevering self-esteem through daily struggles is apparent in how youth present themselves at this school. However, it was this tactic that the school forbid, based on the perception of sneakers as the antith-esis of being a scholar.

The procedure described at this particular high school, of forcing youth to switch shoes, resembles a much larger problem across urban education spaces where youth are forced to take off their authenticity to assimilate to schools' definitions of knowing and being. This narrative is representative of a significant clashing of perception between dominant and marginalized populations with regard to what integrity, healing and commitment to one's development look like. For Black and Brown, who pull from a slew of cultural practices to commit to their own develop-ment, this process looks and feels like schools do not care about their lived experiences and their commitment to being authentically them-selves. In this sense, schools are asking students to forfeit their dignity and self-respect in order to be perceived as respectful, good or profes-sional. Digging deeper, a decision to push students to demonstrate "core values" that can only be achieved through relinquishing who they are is rooted in historical issues in our education system around assimilation, disguised as helping or saving.

The Context of Urban School Counseling

School Counseling and Its Origins

The vast majority of school counseling literature across the last two decades has come to a singular conclusion – the role of the school counselor is still not adequately understood or utilized in schools, leading to missed opportunities to support students' academic, personal/social and career development (Chandler et al., 2018; Campbell & Dahir, 1997; Lieberman, 2004; Moyer, 2011). Calling attention to Emdin (2016) urging of teachers to combat oppression in schools, Dollarhide and Lemberger-Truelove (2018) suggested that school counselors, if they are not intentional about the roles they play, can be used by education systems to perpetuate inequalities. This positionality draws from seminal work labeling school counselors as social justice advocates (Holcomb-McCoy, 2007). A deep dive into the history of the school counseling profession illuminates how far the profession is from truly uprooting systemic issues that impact Black and Brown youth today.

Tracing school counseling back to its origins, it is apparent that the field came into existence out of issues around the United States international rankings in Math and Science (Perry, 1993). In fact, the birth of the school counseling field was a direct response to a dent the United States felt in its national prowess when the Soviet Union launched the Sputnik satellite in 1957. In response, United States passed the National Defense Education Act which spurred a vocational guidance movement specifically aimed at ensuring that (mostly White) young people were being guided into careers in Math and Science. America's educational standing had been dwindling, but a system wide change in an attempt to bolster the academic and vocational pursuits of young people did not begin until the United States felt like they were losing a race publicly (Perry, 1993). A reminder, Black youth were not universally offered schooling until 1968 (Ladson-Billings, 2006), roughly 10 years after this federal push for more school counselors. This is important to note for a couple of reasons. First, the role of school counselor was not originally designed to support students socially or emotionally, or to really understand their lived experiences at all. It was to push them to excel academically and publicly, so the rest of the world could know America was still dominant. Second, the birth of school counseling was not ever about advocating for youth of color, but rather about gathering White men (erroneously framed as the best and the brightest) to represent the United States in math and science fields. These fields today are over-populated with White men (Banchefsky & Park, 2018), and some White women (Miller, Eagly, & Linn, 2015), with significantly less Black and Brown people (Fouad, & Santana, 2017). A seemingly moral and just cause was pursued (more school counselors in schools), for self-serving reasons, while silencing social and emotional concerns and producing racial and gender-based inequities and severely stunted the development of Black and Brown youth. This is our history.

Cultural Competence and Social Justice

Today, school counselors are responsible for supporting students' personal/social, academic and career development (ASCA, 2019). The American School Counselor Association (ASCA, 2019) advocates for the use of a national model for comprehensive school counseling programs in attempt to clearly define the roles, responsibilities and adequate use of school counselors in school. However, school counselors are still struggling to engage in direct academic, career and personal/social development, perhaps because of large caseloads and being tasked with non-school-counseling duties (Kim & Lambie, 2018; Mau, Li, & Hoetmer, 2016). While a third of the school counselor's role is to support students' personal/social development, research suggests that school counselors are more often asked to engage in work that aligns and supports students' academic and career development (Astramovich et al., 2013). Beyond caseload issues, or time allotment, others have expressed that school counselors lack the pre-requisite training to challenge systems of inequity that pervades our education system and marginalizes Black and Brown youth (Holcomb-McCoy, 2007). Scholars in school counseling are split with regard to how they define the school counselors role, with some believing that the roles school counselors play as educators (ASCA, 2019) hinder their ability to function as counselors who support student's mental health (Lambie et al., 2019). Instead, I argue the school counselor must understand how to situate themselves within the education system and then leverage their counseling skills (dialogical and relational) to preventatively work with students toward abolishing problematic educational structures (Love, 2019), and supporting their academic, social/emotional and career development. This preventative, developmental, wellness and social justice focused school counselor pulls from counseling theory as well as a detailed and theoretically sound knowledge and history of the education system to inform how they support students holistically (Levy & Lemberger-Truelove, 2021).

Attempting to do any school counseling task without infusing cultural competence, and social justice, will fail Black and Brown youth. For example, the National Alliance on Mental Health (NAMI, 2015) called preventative social and emotional services as a proactive attempt to mitigate adolescent's future development of diagnosable mental illness, which perhaps explains the sudden calls for Social and Emotional learning in education (Markowitz & Bouffard, 2020). However, emotional wellness concerns are still highest among racial-ethnic minorities (Sun, Hoyt, Brockberg, Lam, & Tiwari, 2016), indicating that even when school counselors are allowed to utilize their counseling skills to aid student's social and emotional development, racial disparities still exist. This reality is not surprising, given that school counselors are trained to use highly westernized approach to counseling (Tao, Owen, Pace, & Imel, 2015; Wendt, Gone, & Nagata, 2015) that fail to provide them with the culturally competent theories and active listening skills needed to combat systems of oppression that marginalize the intersectional identities of Black and Latinx youth (Singh et al., 2020). The real issue with the school counselor's role might simply be preparedness.

Ratts and Greenleaf (2017) posit that in order to be culturally competent, school counseling professionals must learn about individual cultural differences and engage in social justice advocacy. The development of cultural competence is an ever-changing and lifelong process (Ratts et al., 2016), requiring a commitment to social justice and cultural humility (ongoing self-critique, self-reflection and collaboration; Hook et al., 2016). Without a commitment to social justice advocacy and cultural humility, "it is impossible to understand all the intersectionalities that we, our students, and our clients inhabit and enact" (Anastas, 2010, p. 91). Therefore, culturally responsive counseling services require an ecological perspective in which practitioners develop an in-depth understanding of a client's social context and cultural values (McMahon et al., 2014). Practitioners can then make efforts to engage in culturally responsive interventions that target the systemic barriers to a successful healing process (Ratts et al., 2016). In order to combat forms of oppression in current school counseling environments, school counselors need to move away from talk therapy (plagued by problematic power-dynamics) to co-creating interventions with students that address their holistic development (Smith & Chambers, 2015). This shift enables counselors to address aspects of the development process where they have knowledge deficits, specifically in identifying culturally relevant interventions. The partnership with students in the helping relationship allows counselors to accept what they do not know and position the students as the experts of their cultural forms of healing, in order to co-identify a path forward (Smith & Chambers, 2015). When working with Black and Brown youth, school counselors pull from their inherently educational and counseling identity to authentically understand youth's lived experiences, identities and context to co-construct a path toward holistic development.

School Counseling in Contemporary Schooling

A recognizing of the history of the school counseling profession, and of schooling broadly, is a necessary precursor for nurturing youth's development within oppressive schooling systems. To support this development, I argue school counseling practitioners must adopt a practice that pulls from humanistic counseling methodologies that enable youth to give voice to their knowledges, histories and realities. The goal of the humanistic process was to help the client achieve congruence, an alignment between real and ideal self, what (Love, 2016) is referred to as *wholeness*. Rogers (1957) purported that self-actualization is an individual's path toward reaching their full potential as a human, involving the reconciliation of the *real self* and *self image*. An individual's *real self* is the manifestation of their unadulterated thoughts and feelings. In contrast, the *self image* is how individuals see themselves in the world. The more these two selves overlap, the more "congruent" an individual is said to be, and the less distress or "incongruence" the individual is said to have. Incongruence is the birthplace for psychological tension (Sanders & Joseph, 2016). As evidenced in the narrative above, age-old education practices force racially and ethnically diverse youth to abandon their *real selves* in order to obtain an identity that aligned with a *self image* defined by Eurocentric ideals. In this sense, the nature of traditional schooling produces incongruence.

A contemporary school counseling model need to draw from salient beliefs of Rogers's (1957) approach that suggest that 1) the client has all of the answers to their problems within themselves, it is simply the counselor's responsibility to help the client locate and hear those thoughts and 2) the therapeutic relationship between the counselor and client is the chief mechanism in fostering change. These beliefs are guided by the Rogerian core concepts of *congruence, empathy, and unconditional positive regard*. In order for an individual to self-actualize, the counselor must be able to put themselves in the client's shoes and accept and respect their position unconditionally (Rogers, 1957). Calls for a Rogerian approach, particularly in supporting Black and Brown youth who identify with hip-hop, signify a return to the school counselor's skills in building relationships and dialogical listening (Hansen, 2012). During their pre-service clinical training, school counselors are taught and practice basic counseling skills associated with the humanistic approach (CACREP, 2016), but seldom asked to consider how this approach is applied directly in schools (Dollarhide & Lemberger-Truelove, 2018), in culturally competent capacities (Holcomb-McCoy, 2004) or to use them as a means to combat oppressive educational systems that minimize youth's career, academic and social/emotional potential of contemporary youth (Emdin, 2016; Holcomb-McCoy, 2007).

Addressing Oppression

Remaining attuned to systems of inequity is crucial for school counselors in contemporary schools. Inequities are not identified to instill fear, but with an effort to get rid of them, and aid students' authentic expression and development. The lack of school counseling services generally in schools (Carlson & Kees, 2013, Christian & Brown, 2018; DeKruyf et al., 2013), compiled with the lack of culturally sensitive services and systemic factors that threaten authentic self-discovery and social and emotional development, present significant concern regarding adequate mental health support for youth of color. Adolescents who identify as Latinx or Black face unique challenges within the United States and coping strategies become especially important for emotional, physical and social well-being. The experience of stressors related to poverty (Santiago et al., 2016), discrimination (Sirin et al., 2015), forced assimilation (Huq et al., 2016), illuminating the potential value of interventions to ameliorate stressors and to enhance Latinx adolescents' coping repertoires (Santiago et al., 2016). While it is essential to be able to identify and promote the strengths, resilience and the reinforcing value of community for healthy development within the African American community, threats to well-being must be recognized (Love, 2019; Travis & Leech, 2014). For African American high school students, research shows that high levels of discrimination were significantly associated with high levels of perceived stress, and ultimately greater psychological distress (Hughes et al., 2015), correlated with academic and career deficits (Gueldner et al., 2020).

Beyond the lack of time school counselors have to engage in direct counseling work (Mau, Li, & Hoetmer, 2016), assessment of teacher education programs nationally illuminate that social and emotional learning skills and curricula is a significant gap in training (Schonert-Reichl, Kitil, & Hanson-Peterson, 2017), often leaving Black and Brown youth to process emotional stress on their own. Therefore, despite the vast amount of research indicating that adolescents require support in developing coping repertoire to deal with life stressors, educators are underprepared to support students in this capacity. When emotions manifest in classrooms, they are often not met with empathy, unconditional positive regard and a search to understand lived experience and context, but instead young people of color are more likely to be targeted by disproportionate teacher referrals (Villodas et al., 2019) and other discipline practices (Blake et al., 2011; Crenshaw et al., 2015). In support of the claims that oppressive systems work to erase authenticity (Emdin, 2016) students have reported feeling like good students when performing as docile or obedient in classrooms (Baluran & Pido, 2017). Complicit in this reality, school counselors have reported carrying out discipline practices, despite feeling as if they conflicted with their role (Goodman-Scott, 2019). While traditional classroom management practices might aim to produce obedient students (Bridgman, 2018), empowerment-based approaches to addressing student behavior support developing authentic relationships with youth in order to support them in processing difficult emotional concerns (Davis, 2017) and collaborating on the removal of inadequate and inequitable school policies (Love, 2019).

Hip-Hop as The Path Forward

The aforementioned concerns support Emdin's (2016) call for educators to understand modern forms of systemic oppression youth endure in and around school buildings that push for the erasure of their cultural complexities in route to assimilation. Specifically, this lens is necessary in the field of urban school counseling which is populated with youth who identify with hip-hop culture. To actualize school counseling praxis that combats oppressive systems, school counselors pull from their humanistic tenants to trust youth as the holders of the knowledge and insights necessary for healing. By using their dialogical and relational skills to actively listen and learn about youths' stories, identities and contexts, the two parties co-select interventions that assist with student's holistic development. To address contemporary challenges Black and Brown youth face, school counselors must be equipped with culturally responsible approaches to counseling that promote Black and Brown youths' voice. Hip-hop has historically functioned as a medium through which Black and Brown youth in urban spaces express thoughts and feelings and identify and dismantle systems of inequity (Chang, 2005), and has been explored as a culturally responsive approach to school counseling (Levy et al., 2018; Washington, 2018). In this sense, hip-hop is germane to youth voice, and approaches to school counseling that utilize hip-hop will support counselors and students in authentic self-expression, and in the identification of systemic barriers to self-actualization. It is therefore the express purpose of this book to describe a series of research studies that explore a particular approach to hip-hop and school counseling. In Chapter 2 of this book, I explore a particular pilot study where I worked as a school counselor to design, implement and evaluate a hip-hop-based counseling curriculum for small-group counseling and classroom settings.

References

Adjapong, E. (2019). Towards a practice of emancipation in urban schools: A look at student experiences through the science genius battles program. *Journal of Ethnic and Cultural Studies, 6*(1), 15–27.

Adjapong, E. S., & Emdin, C. (2015). Rethinking pedagogy in urban spaces: Implementing hip-hop pedagogy in the urban science classroom. *Journal of Urban Learning, Teaching, and Research, 11*, 66–77.

American School Counselor Association. (2019). *The ASCA national model: A framework for school counseling programs* (4th ed.) Author.

Anastas, J. (2010). *Teaching in social work: An educators' guide to theory and practice.* New York, NY: Columbia University Press.

Anderson, J. D. (2002, February 28). *Historical perspectives on Black academic achievement.* Paper presented for the *Visiting Minority Scholars Series Lecture. Wisconsin Center for Educational Research,* University of Wisconsin, Madison.

Astramovich, R. L., Hoskins, W. J., Gutierrez, A. P., & Bartlett, K. A. (2013). Identifying role diffusion in school counseling. *Professional Counselor, 3*(3), 175–184.

Baluran, C. A., & Pido, R. G. (2017). The oppressive classroom: Student construction of subjectivities. *Asia Pacific Journal of Multidisciplinary Research, 5*(3), 79–86.

Banchefsky, S., & Park, B. (2018). Negative gender ideologies and gender-science stereotypes are more pervasive in male-dominated academic disciplines. *Social Sciences, 7*(2), 27.

Blake, J. J., Butler, B. R., Lewis, C. W., & Darensbourg, A. (2011). Unmasking the inequitable discipline experiences of urban Black girls: Implications for urban educational stakeholders. *The Urban Review, 43*(1), 90–106.

Bridgman, T. (2018). Overcoming compliance to change: Dynamics of power, obedience, and resistance in a classroom restructure. *Management Teaching Review,* 2379298118791106.

Campbell, C. A., & Dahir, C. A. (1997). *The national standards for school counseling programs* (p. 17). Alexandria, VA: American School Counselor Association.

Carlson, L. A., & Kees, N. L. (2013). Mental health services in public schools: A preliminary study of school counselor perceptions. *Professional School Counseling, 16*(4), 2156759X150160401.

Caro, R. A. (1974). *The power broker: Robert Moses and the fall of New York.* Knopf.

Chandler, J. W., Burnham, J. J., Riechel, M. E. K., Dahir, C. A., Stone, C. B., Oliver, D. F., Davis, A.P., & Bledsoe, K. G. (2018). Assessing the counseling and non-counseling roles of school counselors. *Journal of School Counseling, 16*(7), n7.

Chang, J. (2005). *Can't stop won't stop: A history of the hip-hop generation.* New York, NY: St. Martin's Press.

Christian, D. D., & Brown, C. L. (2018). Recommendations for the role and responsibilities of school-based mental health counselors. *Journal of School-Based Counseling Policy and Evaluation,* 1(*1*), 26–39. https://doi.org/10.25774/nmfk-y245

Council for Accreditation of Counseling and Related Educational Programs. (2016). 2016 CACREP standards. Retrieved from http://www.cacrep.org/wp-content/uploads/2018/05/2016-Standards-with-Glossary-5.3.2018.pdf

Crenshaw, K., Ocen, P., & Nanda, J. (2015). Black girls matter: Pushed out, over-policed, and underprotected. https://www.atlanticphilanthropies.org/wp-content/uploads/2015/09/BlackGirlsMatter_Report.pdf

Davis, J. R. (2017). From discipline to dynamic pedagogy: A re-conceptualization of classroom management. *Berkeley Review of Education, 6*(2).

Decker, J. (1993). The state of rap: Time and place in hip-hop nationalism. *Social Text, 34,* 5344.

DeKruyf, L., Auger, R. W., & Trice-Black, S. (2013). The role of school counselors in meeting students' mental health needs: Examining issues of professional identity. *Professional School Counseling, 16*(5), 271–282.

Dollarhide, C. T., & Lemberger-Truelove, M. E. (Eds.). (2018). *Theories of school counseling for the 21st century.* Oxford University Press.

Dunley, T. (2000, May 12). The colour barrier is no more. So whose music is it anyway? *Montreal Gazette*, p. A1.

Emdin, C. (2010). Affiliation and alienation: Hip-hop, rap, and urban science education. *Journal of Curriculum Studies, 42*(1), 1–25. doi:10.1080/00220270903161118

Emdin, C. (2016). *For white folks who teach in the hood… and the rest of y'all too: Reality pedagogy and urban education.* Beacon Press.

Ferg-Cadima, J. (2004, May). Black, White, and Brown: Latino school desegregation efforts in the pre– and post–Brown v. Board of Education era. Washington, DC: Mexican-American Legal Defense and Education Fund.

Forman, M. (2002). "Keeping it real"?: African youth identities and hip hop. In R.A. Young (Ed.) *Music, popular culture, identities* (pp. 89–118). Brill.

Fouad, N. A., & Santana, M. C. (2017). SCCT and underrepresented populations in STEM fields: Moving the needle. *Journal of Career Assessment, 25*(1), 24–39.

Fultz, M. (1995). African American teachers in the South, 1890–1940: Powerlessness and the ironies of expectations and protests. *History of Education Quarterly, 35*(4), 401–422.

Goodman-Scott, E. (2019). Enhancing student learning by "building a caring climate": School Counselors' experiences with classroom management. *Professional School Counseling, 22*(1)

Graham, N. J. (2017). Southern rap and the rhetoric of region. *Phylon (1960-), 54*(2), 41–57.

Gueldner, B. A., Feuerborn, L. L., & Merrell, K. W. (2020). *Social and emotional learning in the classroom: Promoting mental health and academic success.* Guilford Publications.

Hansen, J. T. (2012). Extending the humanistic vision: Toward a humanities foundation for the counseling profession. *The Journal of Humanistic Counseling, 51*(2), 133–144.

Hayes, D. W. (1993). Educating the hip-hop generation: Communication barriers offset efforts to reach young minds. *Black Issues in Higher Education, 10*(14), 30–33.

Hill, M. L. (2009). *Beats, rhymes, and classroom life: Hip-hop pedagogy and the politics of identity.* Teachers College Press.

Holcomb-McCoy, C. (2004). Assessing the multicultural competence of school counselors: A checklist. *Professional School Counseling, 7*(3), 178–186.

Holcomb-McCoy, C. (2007). *School counseling to close the achievement gap: A social justice framework for success.* Corwin Press.

Hook, J. N., Farrell, J. E., Davis, D. E., DeBlaere, C., Van Tongeren, D. R., & Utsey, S. O. (2016). Cultural humility and racial microaggressions in counseling. *Journal of Counseling Psychology, 63*, 269–277. doi:10.1037/cou0000114

Hughes, M., Kiecolt, K. J., Keith, V. M., & Demo, D. H. (2015). Racial identity and well-being among African Americans. *Social Psychology Quarterly, 78*(1), 25–48.

Huq, N., Stein, G. L., & Gonzalez, L. M. (2016). Acculturation conflict among Latino youth: Discrimination, ethnic identity, and depressive symptoms. *Cultural Diversity and Ethnic, Minority Psychology, 22*(3), 377–385. https://doi.org/10.1037/cdp0000070

Kim, N., & Lambie, G. W. (2018). Burnout and implications for professional school counselors. *Professional Counselor, 8*(3), 277–294.

Ladson-Billings, G. (2006). From the achievement gap to the education debt: Understanding achievement in US schools. *Educational Researcher, 35*(7), 3–12.

Lambie, G. W., & Williamson, L. L. (2004). The challenge to change from guidance counseling to professional school counseling: A historical proposition. *Professional School Counseling,* 124–131.

Lambie, G. W., Stickl Haugen, J., Borland, J. R., & Campbell, L. O. (2019). Who Took "Counseling" out of the Role of Professional School Counselors in the United States?. *Journal of School-Based Counseling Policy and Evaluation, 1*(3), 51–61.

Levy, I. (2019). Hip-hop and spoken word therapy in urban school counseling. *Professional School Counseling, 22*(1b). doi:10.1177/2156759X19834436

Levy, I. & Lemberger-Truelove, M.E. (2021). School counselors' situatedness: The influence of the educational setting on roles and responsibilities. *Professional School Counseling.*

Levy, I., Cook, A. L., & Emdin, C. (2018). Remixing the school counselor's tool kit: Hip-hop spoken word therapy and YPAR. *Professional School Counseling, 22*(1). doi:10.1177/2156759X18800285

Lieberman, A. (2004). Confusion regarding school counselor functions: School leadership impacts role clarity. *Education, 124*(3).

Love, B. L. (2016). Anti-Black state violence, classroom edition: The spirit murdering of Black children. *Journal of Curriculum and Pedagogy, 13*(1), 22–25.

Love, B. (2019). *We want to do more than survive: Abolitionist teaching and the pursuit of educational freedom.* Beacon Press.

Markowitz, N. L., & Bouffard, S. M. (2020). *Teaching with a Social, Emotional, and Cultural Lens: A Framework for Educators and Teacher Educators.* Harvard Education Press.

Mau, W. C. J., Li, J., & Hoetmer, K. (2016). Transforming high school counseling: Counselors' roles, practices, and expectations for students' success. *Administrative Issues Journal: Connecting Education, Practice, and Research, 6*(2), 83–95.

McLeod, K. (1999). Authenticity within hip-hop and other cultures threatened with assimilation. *Journal of Communication, 49,* 134–150. doi:10.1111/j.1460-2466.1999.tb02821.x

McMahon, H. G., Mason, E. C., Daluga-Guenther, N., & Ruiz, A. (2014). An ecological model of professional school counseling. *Journal of Counseling & Development, 92*(4), 459–471.

Miller, D. I., Eagly, A. H., & Linn, M. C. (2015). Women's representation in science predicts national gender-science stereotypes: Evidence from 66 nations. *Journal of Educational Psychology, 107*(3), 631.

Moyer, M. (2011). Effects of non-guidance activities, supervision, and student-to-counselor ratios on school counselor burnout. *Journal of School Counseling, 9*(5), n5.

National Alliance on Mental Health. (2015). Mental health by the numbers. Retrieved from https://www.nami.org/learn-more/mental-health-bythe-numbers

Perry, N. S. (1993). School counseling. *Counselor Efficacy: Assessing and Using Counseling Outcome Research,* 37–49.

Powell, C. T. (1991). Rap music: An education with a beat from the street. *The Journal of Negro Education, 60*(3), 245–259.

Ratts, M. J., & Greenleaf, A. T. (2017). Multicultural and social justice counseling competencies: A leadership framework for professional school counselors. *Professional School Counseling, 21*(1b).

Ratts, M. J., Singh, A. A., Nassar-McMillan, S., Butler, S. K., & McCullough, J. R. (2016). Multicultural and social justice counseling competencies: Guidelines for the counseling profession. *Journal of Multicultural Counseling and Development, 44*(1), 28–48.

Reyna, C., Brandt, M., & Tendayi Viki, G. (2009). Blame it on hip-hop: Anti-rap attitudes as a proxy for prejudice. *Group Processes & Intergroup Relations, 12*(3), 361–380.

Rogers, C. R. (1957). The necessary and sufficient conditions of therapeutic personality change. *Journal of Consulting Psychology, 21*(2), 95.

Rose, T. (2008). *The hip hop wars: What we talk about when we talk about hip hop–and why it matters.* Civitas Books.

Sanders, P., & Joseph, S. (2016). Person-centered psychology. In A.M. Wood & J. Johnson (Eds.) *The Wiley handbook of positive clinical psychology* (p. 429).

Santiago, C. D., Brewer, S. K., Fuller, A. K., Torres, S. A., Papadakis, J. L., & Ros, A. M. (2016). Stress, coping, and mood among Latino adolescents: A daily diary study. *Journal of Research on Adolescence, 27*(3), 566–580. https://doi.org/10.1111/jora.12294

Schonert-Reichl, K. A., Kitil, M. J., & Hanson-Peterson, J. (2017). To reach the Students, teach the Teachers: A national scan of teacher preparation and social & emotional learning. A report prepared for CASEL. Collaborative for academic, social, and emotional learning.

Singh, A. A., Appling, B., & Trepal, H. (2020). Using the Multicultural and Social Justice Counseling Competencies to Decolonize Counseling Practice: The Important Roles of Theory, Power, *and Action. Journal of Counseling and Development, 98*(3), 261–271. https://doi.org/10.1002/jcad.12321

Sirin, S. R., Rogers-Sirin, L., Cressen, J., Gupta, T., Ahmed, S. F., & Novoa, A. D. (2015). Discrimination-related stress effects on the development of internalizing symptoms among Latino adolescents. *Child Development, 86*(3), 709–725. https://doi.org/10.1111/cdev.12343

Smith, L. T. (2012). *Decolonizing methodologies: Research and indigenous peoples.* Zed Books.

Smith, L., & Chambers, D. A. (2015). Decolonizing psychological practice in the context of poverty. In R. D. Goodman & P. C. Gorski (Eds.), *Decolonizing multicultural counseling through social justice* (pp. 73–84) Springer.

Stephens, T. T. (1992). An examination of the effect of using rap music as an adjunct to music therapy in group counseling.

Sun, S., Hoyt, W. T., Brockberg, D., Lam, J., & Tiwari, D. (2016). Acculturation and enculturation as predictors of psychological help-seeking attitudes (HSAs) among racial and ethnic minorities: A meta-analytic investigation. *Journal of Counseling Psychology, 63*(6), 617.

Tao, K. W., Owen, J., Pace, B. T., & Imel, Z. E. (2015). A meta-analysis of multicultural competencies and psychotherapy process and outcome. *Journal of Counseling Psychology, 62*(3), 337.

Thompson, K. B. (2016). The negative imagery of hip-hop: A brief analysis. In *Qualitative methods in Africana studies: An interdisciplinary approach to examining Africana phenomena* (p. 329).

Travis, R., & Leech, T. G. (2014). Empowerment-based positive youth development: A new understanding of healthy development for African American youth. *Journal of Research on Adolescence, 24*(1), 93–116. https://doi.org/http://doi.10.1111/jora.12062

Tyack, D. (2004). *Seeking common ground: Public schools in a diverse society.* Harvard University Press.

U.S. Government Printing Office (1896). *Report of the superintendent of Indian schools.* Washington, DC: U.S. Government Printing Office.

Villodas, M. T., Pfiffner, L. J., Moses, J. O., Hartung, C., & McBurnett, K. (2019). The roles of student gender, race, and psychopathology in teachers' identification of students for services. *Children and Youth Services Review, 107* (1), 1–9.

Wang, X. (2012). "I am not a qualified dialect rapper: Constructing hip-hop authenticity in China. *Sociolinguistic Studies, 6,* 333–372. doi:10.1558/sols.v6i2.333

Washington, A. R. (2018). Integrating hip-hop culture and rap music into social justice counseling with black males. *Journal of Counseling & Development, 96*(1), 97–105. doi:10.1002/jcad.12181

Wendt, D. C., Gone, J. P., & Nagata, D. K. (2015). Potentially harmful therapy and multicultural counseling: Bridging two disciplinary discourses. *The Counseling Psychologist, 43*(3), 334–358.

Yousman, B. (2003). Blackophilia and blackophobia: White youth, the consumption of rap music, and white supremacy. *Communication Theory, 13*(4), 366–391.

2 Introducing the Pilot Program
A Hip-Hop Lyricism Course

Hip-Hop in School Counseling

The early implementation of HHSWT was built on the assumption that hip-hop offers school counselors a culturally relevant approach that both targets external systems of oppression and supports youth development. Approaches to school counseling that empower youth to function as leaders in the counseling process have been championed as a means to counter-cultural inequities (Cook & Krueger-Henney, 2017; Smith & Chambers, 2015), and hip-hop holds promise in empowering youth (Travis et al., 2019). In order to ensure that all youth are offered direct school counseling services, school counselors are asked to differentiate their curriculum in individual, small-group and classroom instruction settings. Therefore, the school counselor's ability to draw from culturally responsive pedagogy and counseling in classrooms is imperative. However, courses on evidence-based practices for classroom pedagogy in school counseling master programs are sparse at best (Zyromski et al., 2018). Most often, preparation for school counselors to engage in classroom counseling entails lesson plan development (Lopez & Mason, 2017), or classroom management strategies (Goodman-Scott, 2019), but seemingly no research exists exploring school counselor's understanding of pedagogical theory and practice. As counselors, situated within educational contexts, school counselors must be able to simultaneously pull from hip-hop-based counseling and educational frameworks. This chapter will explore a small pilot study that assesses the simultaneous hip-hop-based counseling and pedagogical strategies.

Hip-hop and Spoken Word Therapy

Hip-hop interventions are suggested to offer Black and Latinx youth a platform to explore social and emotional concerns and process inequities (Emdin, Adjapong, & Levy, 2016). Scholars explore both the empowering and risky engagement of Hip-hop culture, but the evidence strongly suggests Hip-hop music can have a positive impact on the well-being of adolescents (Travis & Bowman, 2015). Travis et al. (2019) suggested that a Hip-hop, empowerment and beat-making model in group work might be effective as a strategy to support youth in improving their mental health. HHSWT was theoretically developed as a culturally responsive counseling methodology rooted in evidence-based approaches to counseling such as cognitive behavioral therapy, person-centered therapy, music therapy and bibliotherapy. HHSWT was originally theorized as an individual and group counseling framework where counselors could support youth in exploring difficult emotional experiences for the purpose of then converting the affective and cognitive content of the discussion into hip-hop songs. The development of HHSWT over time has thoroughly examined varying hip-hop cultural processes, and how those might be used inside schools. For instance, HHSWT offers counselors a set of hip-hop-centered tools that they can use in the counseling process to support youth in writing, recording and performing songs about difficult thoughts and feelings. These tools include the hip-hop cypher to support group process and sharing (Levy et al., 2018b), creating emotionally themed mixtapes (Levy et al., 2018a), lyric writing as emotive journaling and dyadic song collaboration as role-play (Levy, 2019). Each of these HHSWT techniques offers a culturally salient process where youth of color can disclose and process difficult thoughts and feelings with their counselor and are explored within the context of a school counseling curriculum later in this chapter.

Reality Pedagogy

To support school counselors in adapting their small-group counseling curriculum to classroom settings, I pull from Reality pedagogy (RP; Emdin, 2011) which is humanistic in nature, designed to foster attunement with youth's cultural worldviews. RP is an approach to teaching and learning in urban schools designed to provide youth with the agency to actively engage in classrooms where they traditionally underperform (Emdin, 2011). Its chief goal is to acknowledge the varying standpoints of students in the classroom and use information gleaned from students as the point from which pedagogy is birthed. RP uses hip-hop culture and its focus on privileged voice to allow music and other forms of cultural expression. RP functions to provide teachers with a set of practical tools for meeting its goals including co-generative dialogues, co-teaching, cosmopolitanism, context, content and competition (Emdin, 2011). For example, co-generative dialogues are a series of conversations educators have with a small group of students outside of the classroom to troubleshoot issues in the classroom and co-create interventions. Counselors engaging in hip-hop-based classroom counseling setting might meet with a small group of students to discuss different emotional themes they believe the class would want to write about, or specific artists/music students would like to listen to or analyze as a group. Solutions found in co-generative dialogues are then used in co-teaching, where students are then asked to reimagine one of the counselor's classroom counseling lesson plans as homework, to tailor it to the cultural worldviews of their peers and then teach that lesson.

Together HHSWT and RP serve as an approach to school counseling, which supports Black and Brown youth in exploring their lived experiences in culturally sensitive and authentic capacities. In the following section, I explore a particular pilot study where I worked as a school counselor to design, implement and evaluate a hip-hop-based group counseling curriculum within a classroom instruction setting. This pilot study sought to assess student outcomes with regards to stress, analyzing whether or not hip-hop approaches to group work could result in stress reduction or the fostering of emotional stress coping skills. The curriculum for this pilot program is discussed to showcase the practical use of HHSWT and RP. A summary of the study's findings is also provided, as a basis to draw implications for the future evaluation of HHSWT in school counseling practice.

Exploring a 2016–2017 Pilot Study

During the 2016–2017 academic year, I was working as a school counselor at an Urban High School in New York City, where I developed, implemented and evaluated a HHSWT group counseling intervention in a classroom setting. A formal study published in the Professional School Counseling journal (Levy, 2019), examined this work, and is extrapolated upon here. The hip-hop curriculum aimed to increase students' level of comfort for engaging in self-reflection, emotional exploration and for accessing counseling services overall. In addition, it was the goal of the curriculum to aid students in developing stress coping skills. My principal and me identified these goals as relevant to my caseload, and as aligned with research suggesting emotional stress is a mental health concern that adolescents should process with their school counselors (Lindsey et al., 2018; Mason et al., 2017; Lambie et al., 2019).

Hip-hop and Spoken Word Therapy Course

The HHSWT curriculum was designed for a counseling group. However, given my workload as a school counselor at this urban high school, it was difficult to run groups regularly. Oftentimes I would find groups interrupted by meetings, clerical work or student crises. In attempt to circumvent this concern, I pitched the idea of a hip-hop lyricism class to my principal as an arts elective for students (which was required for graduation). As a school counselor, it is our responsibility to both advocate for the proper use of our role (Beck & Lane, 2019) and for resources to students support our students (Ratts & Greenleaf, 2018). Adjusting school counseling curriculum to be deployed in a classroom setting is also part of the school counselor's role as instructors (ASCA, 2019). While it is not necessarily feasible to suggest that all school counselors apply to teach elective classes as counseling groups, there is a larger argument to be made that school counselors need assess how their individual school treats their role, as well as what their caseload of students need, and then develop appropriate methods to advocating for their role and students. Given an understanding that emotional stressors were prevalent for students on my caseload and that I would not have time to run a traditional 10- to 12-week counseling group, functioning as an instruction enabled me to teach a hip-hop lyric writing course as an elective, and allowed me time to utilize a small-group curriculum which targeted students emotional stress. For this course, students met every other day for 50 minutes for an entire school year.

Designing Course Curriculum

As the school counselor, I was in charge of both designing and facilitating the hip-hop lyricism course curriculum. This curriculum was also developed using the HHSWT as the counseling framework and also by using RP (Emdin, 2016) as the pedagogical framework. The class was designed to run like a counseling group, where the content was co-developed by students. Most of the course lessons in the curriculum were pre-constructed to adequately engage students in discussing, writing, recording and performing hip-hop lyrics about previously determined emotional themes.

Focus on Emotional Themes

However, given the priority placed on the co-development of content with students, the course included students co-teaching lessons – as an element that followed from Emdin's (2016) reality pedagogy; consistent with this, the course instructor also worked with students outside of class time so as to assist them in the design of lessons the students were to co-teach; these lessons were typically focused upon emotional themes of their choosing. Another aspect of the curriculum, also followed the work of Emdin (2016), specifically with regard to allocating time and space within the curriculum for students and the course facilitator to engage in co-generative dialogues; within these co-generative dialogues, the students and facilitator worked together to troubleshoot any emergent issues in the class. This was designed to keep the class on track in accomplishing the overall course goal: i.e., for students to create an album/CD of songs (i.e., in hip-hop known as "tracks") that covered all the emotional themes they deemed relevant to their lives. This allowed students to use their reality and life context to support learning in the classroom (Emdin, 2016).

The course curriculum also had elements rooted in the person-centered constructs of HHSWT (Levy, 2012) that had been inspired by the work of Rogers (1957). More specifically, the aim was for writing lyrics to support the expression of emotion, as well as uncover the answers to their own problems (Levy, 2012). The course curriculum included several lessons designed to target specific emotions that the school counselor believed students were already experiencing. Also, students were encouraged to write about emotions and situations that they felt had an impact on their school performance, and to use lyric writing to foster thoughts and feelings about their career development. The curriculum was designed so that, during each group session the instructor would facilitate a conversation around a given emotional theme (e.g., self-doubt, home life, interpersonal drama, etc.); and students were encouraged to write about that theme. After conversing with students, the counselor would put a beat on, encourage students to *write* and provide prompts through words/phrases related to the topic, as the students wrote. A handful of tactics were developed, based on HHSWT, to address students writing and prepare them for the recording process.

The use of hip-hop lyric writing in a journal, as a form of Beck's (1963) homework assignments, was deployed regularly. Indeed, each student was given a spiral notebook to facilitate this process. Students were asked to turn in their notebooks to the course instructor every time they experienced a difficult emotion outside of class. By asking students to update others at the start of class on new writings as a "check-in", the course instructor allowed for students outside of class lyric writing to potentially become the focus of any given group. This was also a therapeutic approach that allowed for students to share any new stressful or emotional event that had arisen in their lives, while attention and time was focused on their update. This use of the "check-in" also led to regular meaningful dialogues between the course facilitator and students.

Use of Group Activities

The course also included group activities. For example, there was the experience of regular group critiques of student lyrics. There was also the use of student collaboration, including the group being engaged in role-play, following the work of Bandura (1986, 1997). Through the use of role play, it was believed that students would learn to analyze thoughts and feelings and reframe faulty cognitions. Further, in certain lessons students were asked to work in small groups to co-construct songs around emotional experiences they all had in common. This was designed to allow students the chance to further role-play certain emotional experiences. This process was also deployed in an attempt to allow students an opportunity to relate to one another, feel less alone in their struggle and work together to troubleshoot responses when working on any given emotional theme. Throughout the course of the year, co-generative dialogues were used as a means for the class to evaluate the progress of their class mixtape, to address any concerns they had about the functionality of the class, their progress and general ability to work together. The course had a culminating closing event. Specifically, the course culminated in a final hip-hop showcase held at the school. At this event, students performed their written and recorded hip-hop songs, and then released the songs online.

Final Comment on the Curriculum

Beginning with the design of an authentic studio space and encompassing the design of a course curriculum rooted in varied models and concepts (i.e., Bandura, 1986, 1997; Beck, 1963; Emdin, 2016; Levy, 2012; Rogers, 1957), there was a deliberate approach to meeting the course goal. This included providing students with a sense of freedom to engage in the process of lyric writing, recording, performing – while also achieving their own personal therapeutic outcomes, as they improved in their ability to cope with their emotions and any related stress. The school principal, in supporting the establishment of this pioneering hip-hop lyricism course, had hoped that students would learn to identify specific stressors that impacted their lives in a negative fashion, while facilitating students arriving at tangible solutions for overcoming and coping with these stressors. Hence, the school principal provided the permission for a secondary analysis of a body of data that the school had accumulated (i.e., participant survey, focus group data, lyrics on recordings) in order to support an evaluation of the hip-hop lyricism course.

Relevant Methods

The hip-hop lyricism course had two sections of six students, each section occurring every other day. Therefore 12 total participants were randomly selected from a group of 30 students who indicated on a school-wide course elective sign-up sheet that they wanted to take the hip-hop lyricism course. Capping each section of the course at six students was in alignment with recommending sizing for small groups with high school

aged youth (DeLucia-Waack, 2006). Of the 12 participants, half identified as Black and 9 were identified as male.

A mixed-methods analysis was used by the school counselor to evaluate the effectiveness of the course including a pre- and post-course survey, a post-course focus group and an analysis of student lyrics. The
pre-course survey contained a total of three scales, which assessed emotional coping, emotional self-awareness and stress. Transcripts of the
focus group and student lyrics were collected to assess how promoting
youth voice (i.e., hip-hop) in counseling might support their social and
emotional development. A phenomenological approach was used by the
school counselor in qualitative analysis to explore the students' world
and subjective experiences (Creswell, 2013; Lincoln & Guba, 1985).

Pilot Study Findings

Quantitative data analysis explored changes in student's emotional self-
awareness, perceived stress and stress coping skill development. The
main quantitative finding suggested that the student sample's pre-course
stage of change for coping with emotional stress mean score of 2.94, or
at the contemplation level for using emotional stress coping strategies,
significantly increased to a mean score of 4.03, indicating students were
taking action to cope with emotional stress (Levy, 2019). While, no
statistically significant differences were found with regard to student's
emotional self-awareness, or perceived stress, mean score differences for
both variables from pre- to post-course found, noting decreased
perceived stress and increased emotional self-awareness as a result of
participating in this course (Levy, 2019).

With regard to the qualitative analysis (student lyrics and focus group
interviews), three overarching categories emerged suggesting students:
1) demonstrated increased emotional self-awareness, 2) developed a
newly learned coping skill and 3) developed a stronger self-image. For
the first category, student lyrics and focus groups supported the
conclusion that students demonstrated increased emotional self-
awareness, with a specific sub-theme indicating student's willingness to
be *open with their feelings*. A student quote from a focus group that
exemplified this theme was:

> Basically that's just another way of expressing myself, how other
> people write books or whatever, write poems, I write raps. Raps
> has helped, just helped bring me out of a little shell that I'm com-
> fortable with, and get more in touch with my emotions.

The second category contained student focus group comments and lyrics suggesting they developed new coping skills. Analyses also brought

forth three sub-themes, or coping skills: Writing through stress, cathartic writing and reflective writing. An example of a student lyric that justified writing through stress was,

> I get mad and then want to swing,/I'm sorry to be so angry and violent./Trying not to curse but it's on the tip of my tongue,/and when it slips out I am ready to run./But I'm not running, no not today./Cause now you gonna listen to what I have to say.

Cathartic writing contained student quotes like, *"Writing lyrics, it comes from within us. Something that we've been holding in, that's what I like about this class, that it was to let all of that out, and it feels good."* Reflective writing was exemplified by student quotes, such as, *"We could always learn from our past and like you said, embrace it, no matter what it was. That's why I love writing about my past."* Each student quote or lyric under the category of developing coping skills suggested that students were able to use lyric writing, and the hip-hop lyricism course more broadly, to navigate stress, for personal catharsis and to reflect on and process past experiences.

The final category developed from focus group quotes and lyrics indicated that students developed a stronger self-image. This category was further substantiated by two sub-themes: a) Empowerment and Voice: Realizing the value of their own voice and b) Advocacy and Agency: Becoming advocates for social justice issues. Evidence for student's feeling empowered, or realizing the value of their own voice, contained quotes such as, *"Yeah I'm Black so they doubt that I can make it honestly,/I promise Imma major in forensic anthropology, or criminology, and ain't nobody stoppin' me"*. Advocacy and Agency on the other hand, was of quotes like *"Yeah I focus my lyrics on issues in society, racism, and police brutally like all the things I see. I expose them."*

Salient Learnings

The purpose of this study was to determine the impact of a hip-hop lyricism course, as a school counseling intervention, on students' social and emotional development. Most notably, quantitative analysis suggested that through participating in the hip-hop lyricism course, students moved from preparation stage for emotional coping to an action stage. Research suggests that individuals who report being in the action stage for developing a new behavior are likely to maintain that behavior (Horiuchi et al., 2010). This finding was supported by the qualitative data as well, which offered additional evidence that students developed a more robust coping repertoire as a result of participating in the hip-hop lyricism course. Both the quantitative and qualitative findings support the idea that HHSWT be used by counselors who wish to address the need for Black and Latinx youth to develop coping strategies for variety of stressors they face (Sanchez et al., 2013; Santiago, et al., 2017), and the ASCA (2019) personal/social outcomes of demonstrating effective coping skills for dealing with problems. Results also are suggestive of the school counselor's use of classroom instruction as an effective medium to meet the personal/social needs of youth (ASCA, 2019; Lemberger et al., 2018). Further, when engaging in classroom-based counseling work, there is value in integrating pedagogical theory and practice such as reality pedagogy (Emdin, 2016).

In attempting to support student's social and emotional development, my principal hoped the HHSWT course would support students' emotional-coping skills. While research has shown that adolescent boys are less likely to express emotion in comparison to adolescent girls (Gresham & Gullone, 2012), the HHSWT course enabled a mostly male sample (75% male) to appear emotionally self-aware. Garber et al. (2016) suggested that self-reflection among adolescents was positively associated with problem solving and cognitive restructuring. Park et al. (2016) further suggested that "reflecting over negative experiences from a self-distanced perspective facilitates adaptive self-reflection by changing the way people cognitively represent negative experiences" (p. 2). In this study, under this category, there were relevant coping skill development sub-themes that are reminiscent of that finding: showing ability to self-reflect on past experiences and developing awareness of personal obstacles. Huq et al. (2016) indicated that adolescents' problematic experiences with family and peers led to interpersonal stress. Also, interpersonal stress was a significant predictor of depressive symptoms (Huq et al., 2016). The current study found under this category the sub-theme of processing conflict-ridden interpersonal experiences. Students' ability to reflect on feelings and cultivate awareness of personal obstacles is consistent for the desired ASCA (2014) student personal and social competency of identifying and expressing feelings.

The finding of Self-Image suggests students were able to develop a deeper confidence in themselves and their cultural background through participating in this course. This finding speaks to the importance of allowing youth culture and experiences to enter the classroom (Emdin, 2016) and lyric writing as a medium to explore themselves emotionally (Tyson 2002, Travis and Deepak, 2011). In supporting students' personal and social development, Ratts et al. (2007) called for school counselors to support students' exploration of the various systems (i.e., environmental factors) that oppress them and hinder their development. The sub-theme of becoming advocates for social justice demonstrates that students were able to develop skills to process forms of oppression in the hip-hop lyric writing course with the school counselor, which is also the aim of school counselors working with Black and Brown youth (Emdin,

2016). In discussing HHSWT, Levy (2012) stressed that "the purpose is to assist the client in moving from living in an insecure world to living with a mindset of high self-esteem and authenticity devoid of cognitive distortion and denial of real self" (p. 221).

The Future of HHSWT

This pilot study has implications for school counselors aiming to support student social and emotional development through small-group or classroom-based counseling. Despite the small sample size of this pilot study, the combination of quantitative and qualitative offers support for the use of HHSWT to effectively foster student's coping skills for stress, development of an authentic self-image and emotional self-awareness. School counselors looking to deploy culturally sensitive approaches to counseling, to counter traditional counseling frameworks whose acultural nature might isolate Black and Latinx youth (Tao et al., 2015), should consider using HHSWT. When engaging in classroom-based counseling work, an understanding of how to integrate reality pedagogy might bolster the effectiveness of HHSWT. As such, there is value in training teachers and counselors in the use of HHSWT and Reality Pedagogy. In future research, there should be a larger evaluation of the hip-hop lyricism writing course, using a much larger sample size.

The pilot study described in this chapter evaluated a HHSWT school counseling intervention at an urban youth in the Northeast. While the findings of this study are powerful, the study reported solely on student outcomes. An examination of the HHSWT course as the treatment in a pre–post design might have overshadowed specific components of the course that were more generative of student outcomes. Therefore, in reflecting on this pilot study, I identified a handful of questions. These include: Did the relationships I built with students as a school counselor impact the results? Did the construction of a hip-hop studio as the office for group counseling impact outcomes? Were there curricular choices that were particularly beneficial in producing student outcomes? As a school counselor, did I possess a set of hip-hop-based counseling skills that enabled students to engage in the group process? Can those skills be replicated or learned? Each of these larger questions became the basis for a research agenda that sought to substantiate HHSWT as an approach. In the remainder of this text, I will explore each of these components in individual chapters. These aspects of the HHSWT model include: 1) HHSWT and the therapeutic alliance, 2) HHSWT and counseling office construction, 3) Emotional themed mixtape making in HHSWT, 4) Hip-hop cyphers in HHSWT and 5) Developing HHSWT-based counseling skills.

References

American School Counseling Association. (2019). *The ASCA national model: A framework for school counseling programs* (4th ed.). Alexandria: Author.

American School Counselor Association. (2014). Mindsets and behaviors for student success: K-12 college- and career-readiness standards for every student. Author. https://schoolcounselor.org/asca/ media/asca/home/ MindsetsBehaviors.pdf

Bandura, A. (1986). Fearful expectations and avoidant actions as coeffects of perceived self-inefficacy.

Bandura, A. (1997). The anatomy of stages of change. *American Journal of Health Promotion: AJHP, 12*(1), 8–10.

Beck, A. T. (1963). Thinking and depression: I. Idiosyncratic content and cognitive distortions. *Archives of General Psychiatry, 9*(4), 324–333. doi:10.1001/ archpsyc.1963.01720160014002

Beck, M. J., & Lane, E. M. (2019). Exploring effective practitioner advocacy: A study of ASCA's school counselor of the year finalists. *Journal of Counselor Leadership and Advocacy, 6*(2), 174–187.

Cook, A. L., & Krueger-Henney, P. (2017). Group work that examines systems of power with young people: Youth participatory action research. *The Journal for Specialists in Group Work, 42*(2), 176–193.

Creswell, J. W. (2013). *Qualitative inquiry and research design: Choosing among five approaches.* Los Angeles, CA: Sage.

DeLucia-Waack, J. L. (2006). *Leading psychoeducational groups for children and adolescents.* Sage Publications.

Emdin, C. (2011). Moving beyond the boat without a paddle: Reality pedagogy, Black youth, and urban science education, *The Journal of Negro Education, 80*(3), 284-295. https://www.jstor.org/stable/41341134

Emdin, C. (2016). *For White folks who teach in the hood... and the rest of y'all too: Reality pedagogy and urban education.* Beacon Press.

Emdin, C. (2010). *Urban science education for the hip-hop generation.* Brill Sense.

Emdin, C., Adjapong, E., & Levy, I. (2016). Hip-hop based interventions as pedagogy/therapy in STEM: A model from urban science education. *Journal for Multicultural Education, 10*(3), 307–321. doi:10.1108/JME-03-2016-0023

Garber, J., Frankel, S. A., & Herrington, C. G. (2016). Developmental demands of cognitive behavioral therapy for depression in children and adolescents: Cognitive, social, and emotional processes. *Annual Review of Clinical Psychology, 12*, 181–216.

Goodman-Scott, E. (2019). Enhancing student learning by "building a caring climate": School counselors' experiences with classroom management. *Professional School Counseling, 22*(1).

Gresham, D., & Gullone, E. (2012). Emotion regulation strategy use in children and adolescents: The explanatory roles of personality and attachment. *Personality and Individual Differences, 52*(5), 616–621.

Horiuchi, S., Tsuda, A., Kim, E., Hong, K. S., Park, Y. S., & Kim, U. (2010). Relationships between stage of change for stress management behavior and perceived stress and coping. *Japanese Psychological Research, 52*(4), 291–297.

Huq, N., Stein, G. L., & Gonzalez, L. M. (2016). Acculturation conflict among Latino youth: Discrimination, ethnic identity, and depressive symptoms. *Cultural Diversity and Ethnic Minority Psychology, 22*(3), 377.

Lambie, G. W., Stickl Haugen, J., Borland, J. R., & Campbell, L. O. (2019). Who Took "Counseling" out of the Role of Professional School Counselors in the United States?. *Journal of School-Based Counseling Policy and Evaluation, 1*(3), 51–61.

Lemberger, M. E., Carbonneau, K. J., Selig, J. P., & Bowers, H. (2018). The role of social emotional mediators on middle school students' academic growth as fostered by an evidence-based intervention. *Journal of Counseling & Development, 96*(1), 27–40.

Levy, I. (2019). Hip-hop and spoken word therapy in urban school counseling. *Professional School Counseling, 22*(1b), 27–40. doi:10.1177/2156759X19834436

Levy, I. (2012). Hip hop and spoken word therapy with urban youth. *Journal of Poetry Therapy, 25*(4), 219–224. doi:10.1080/08893675.2012.736182

Levy, I., Cook, A. L., & Emdin, C. (2018a). Remixing the school counselor's tool kit: Hip-hop spoken word therapy and YPAR. *Professional School Counseling, 22*(1). doi:10.1177/2156759X18800285

Levy, I., Emdin, C., & Adjapong, E. S. (2018b). Hip-hop cypher in group work. *Social Work with Groups, 41*(1–2), 103–110. doi:10.1080/01609513.2016.1275265

Levy, I. (2018). Hip-hop and spoken word therapy in urban school counseling. *Professional School Counseling, 22*(1b). doi:10.1177/2156759X19834436

Lopez, C. J., & Mason, E. C. (2017). School counselors as curricular leaders: A content analysis of ASCA lesson plans. *Professional School Counseling, 21*(1b).

Lincoln, Y. G., & Guba, E. (1985). Naturalistic inquiry. London, Sage Publications. Contextualization: Evidence from distributed teams. *Information Systems Research, 16*(1), 9–27.

Lindsey, L., Robertson, P., & Lindsey, B. (2018). Expressive arts and mindfulness: Aiding adolescents in understanding and managing their stress. *Journal of Creativity in Mental Health, 13*(3), 288–297.

Mason, E. C. M., Springer, S. I., & Pugliese, A. (2017). Staff development as a school climate intervention to support transgender and gender nonconforming students: An integrated research partnership model for school counselors and counselor educators. *Journal of LGBT issues in counseling, 11*(4), 301–318.

Mau, W. C. J., Li, J., & Hoetmer, K. (2016). Transforming high school counseling: Counselors' roles, practices, and expectations for students' success. *Administrative Issues Journal: Connecting Education, Practice, and Research, 6*(2), 83–95.

Park, J., Ayduk, Ö., & Kross, E. (2016). Stepping back to move forward: Expressive writing promotes self-distancing. *Emotion, 16*(3), 349.

Ratts, M. J., DeKruyf, L., & Chen-Hayes, S. F. (2007). The ACA advocacy competencies: A social justice advocacy framework for professional school counselors. *Professional School Counseling, 11*(2).

Ratts, M. J., & Greenleaf, A. T. (2018). Counselor–advocate–scholar model: Changing the dominant discourse in counseling. *Journal of Multicultural Counseling and Development, 46*(2), 78–96.

Rogers, C. R. (1957). The necessary and sufficient conditions of therapeutic personality change. *Journal of consulting psychology, 21*(2), 95.

Sanchez, Y. M., Lambert, S. F., & Cooley-Strickland, M. (2013). Adverse life events, coping and internalizing and externalizing behaviors in urban African American youth. *Journal of Child and Family Studies, 22*(1), 38–47.

Santiago, C. D., Brewer, S. K., Fuller, A. K., Torres, S. A., Papadakis, J. L., & Ros, A. M. (2017). Stress, coping, and mood among Latino adolescents: A daily diary study. *Journal of Research on Adolescence, 27*(3), 566–580.

Smith, L., & Chambers, D. A. (2015). Decolonizing psychological practice in the context of poverty. In R. D. Goodman & P. C. Gorski (Eds.), *Decolonizing multicultural counseling through social justice* (pp. 73–84) Springer.

Tao, K. W., Owen, J., Pace, B. T., & Imel, Z. E. (2015). A meta-analysis of multicultural competencies and psychotherapy process and outcome. *Journal of Counseling Psychology, 62*(3), 337–350. doi:10.1037/cou0000086

Travis Jr, R., & Bowman, S. W. (2015). Validation of the individual and community empowerment inventory: A measure of Rap music engagement among first-year college students. *Journal of Human Behavior in the Social Environment, 25*(2), 90–108.

Travis, R., Gann, E., Crooke, A. H., & Jenkins, S. M. (2019). Hip-hop, empowerment, and therapeutic beat-making: Potential solutions for summer learning loss, depression, and anxiety in youth. *Journal of Human Behavior in the Social Environment, 29*(6), 744–765.

Travis, R., Jr., & Deepak, A. (2011). Empowerment in context: Lessons from hip-hop culture for social work practice. *Journal of Ethnic & Cultural Diversity in Social Work, 20*(3), 203–222. doi:10.1080/15313204.2011.594993

Tyson, E. H. (2002). Hip hop therapy: An exploratory study of a rap music intervention with at-risk and delinquent youth. *Journal of Poetry Therapy, 14*(3), 131–144. doi: 10.1023/A:1019795911358

Zyromski, B., Dimmitt, C., Mariani, M., & Griffith, C. (2018). Evidence-based school counseling: Models for integrated practice and school counselor education. *Professional School Counseling, 22*(1.

3 The Importance of "Realness" for a Hip-Hop School Counselor

Reflecting back on the effectiveness of the pilot Hip-hop and Spoken Word Therapy (HHSWT) program, I am left wondering how the relationships I had built with students impacted both the counseling process and outcomes. Therefore, this chapter explores how HHSWT can offer school counselors a platform to develop strong counseling relationships with youth, specifically by interrogating the concept of realness or authenticity in both hip-hop and counseling. Hip-hop culture researchers have documented that "there is perhaps no more fundamental and no more contested principle in Hip-hop than keeping it real" (Kruse, 2016, p. 53). Concurrently, when considering the establishment of a counseling relationship, Rogers (1961) noted:

> "It is only by providing the genuine reality which is in me, that the other person can successfully seek for the reality in him. I have found this to be true when the attitudes I feel are not attitudes with which I am pleased, or attitudes which seem conducive to a good relationship. It seems extremely important to be *real*." (p. 33)

Therefore, notions of realness are of critical importance in both hip-hop culture and the counselor's development and practice.

In hip-hop culture, to keep it real, or authentic, is at the core of what it means to be a successful participant (Neal, 2012). While it is important for participants in hip-hop culture to have art-based skills (rhyming, dancing, designing, tagging, DJing, etc.) scholars have concluded that, despite skill, producing art that is a genuine reflection of who the artist is and their lived experiences takes precedence (Wang, 2012). Emdin (2010) posited that the construction and performance of hip-hop lyrics "connects the histories of the marginalized, echoes their pain, and concurrently articulates the stance of new people who either have been or are being, marginalized in different spaces around the globe" (Emdin, 2010, p. 5). The hip-hop community lives by the ideology of *Real Recognize Real*, a mechanism through which realness can be detected, in order to only affiliate themselves with individuals whom they believe will understand their oppression (Emdin, 2016). A school counselor's ability to form strong relationships with youth, with a particular attunement to realness, is necessary when they intend to critically understand the oppression that Black and Brown youth face. The criteria for the establishment and maintenance of realness are multi-dimensional (McLeod, 1999) and will be explored in this chapter.

Realness in Counseling

When considering realness in the counseling relationship, there is evidence that youth of color doubt the authenticity of counseling professionals (Lindsey & Marcell, 2012). Specifically, Black and Brown youth report being skeptical of seeking help from mental health professionals (Earl, Williams, & Anglade, 2011; Lindsey, Chambers, Pohle, Beall, & Lucksted, 2013; Lindsey & Marcell, 2012; Watkins, Walker, & Griffith, 2010), due to feelings of distrust (Alvidrez, Snowden, & Kaiser, 2008). Feelings of distrust might well be related to research suggesting that Black and Brown youth often do not find counselors relatable and indicate difficulties disclosing information as a result (Lindsey & Marcell, 2012). This research is surprising given that the Rogerian principles at the foundation of the counseling profession explicitly focus on empathic understanding and connection to support the client's emotional disclosure (Aubrey, 1977), and inform the design of counselor training programs (Manzano Boulton, & Davis, 2019; Teding van Berkhout, & Malouff, 2016). Conversely, scholars have detailed that modern counseling professionals have shifted away from a focus on building genuine relationships with clients to the use of techniques and/or interventions (Hansen, Speciale, & Lemberger, 2014) which might illuminate why youth feel disconnected from counselors.

In sum, this unique attunement to authenticity in hip-hop (Emdin, 2010; McLeod, 1999) provides us with a valuable lens or conceptual framework through which we might assess the existence or lack thereof authenticity in the counseling relationship. Therefore, the purpose of this chapter is to demonstrate the utility of the HHSWT as a relational tool, which school counselors can use to respond to the lack of realness or authenticity Black youth feel within counseling relationships.

The Importance of Authenticity

When discussing this HHSWT publicly across the last decade, I have consistently received two types of authenticity-centered questions from interested school counselors. These included: 1) "If I know nothing about hip-hop, can I do this work?" and 2) "As a White person, how can I do this work and not appropriate hip-hop culture?" Both of these questions hold significant value and must be explored, in depth, by counselors in order to establish a strong therapeutic alliance. My answer to these questions has been to urge counselors to sit with those exact questions. I argue that asking oneself these two questions enables us to engage in the self-exploration about our readiness to "keep it real", necessary to use hip-hop-based interventions.

To begin self-exploration in this regard, we must return to humanistic principles which tell us that a) our clients hold the necessary knowledge for change to occur, we are simply responsible for allowing them to see and hear that knowledge and b) if we cannot be authentic in session, then our clients cannot either. In this sense, one does not have to be able to perform hip-hop, or pretend to understand hip-hop more than they do, in order to effectively use HHSWT. In fact, the opposite is true. The more counselors are able to admit that they do not know, the more they can allow their clients to bring their authentic selves, knowledge and expertise into the counseling process. In this sense, I argue that a thorough grounding in humanistic principles, as well as an analysis of cultural appropriation as a construct that impacts one's readiness to keep it real in the counseling relationship, enables the use of HHSWT as a relationship-bolstering tool.

Core Humanistic Conditions

As a counseling framework, HHSWT is rooted in Rogerian concepts of authenticity or congruence, warmth or unconditional positive and empathetic understanding. These core conditions beget the establishment of a strong therapeutic relationship (Rogers, 1957). Essential in a therapeutic relationship is the notion of a clinician being their real, authentic, self. Gelso (2009) theorized that the "real relationship" in psychotherapy is "the personal relationship existing between two or more people as reflected in the degree to which each is genuine with the other and perceives and experiences the other in ways that befit the other" (p. 256–255). Humanists believe that a therapeutic relationship cannot be established with youth of color without the counselor developing the critical awareness and cultural competence necessary see their clients "in the context of their lived experiences to better understand the impact of self and the social barriers in place" (Hannon and Vereen, 2016, p. 241).

A specific focus on context requires counselors understand the intersectionality of Black male client's identities (LaMantia, Wagner, & Bohecker, 2015) and engage in their own self-exploration to shed biases that hinder authentic perceptions of said identities (Hannon & Vereen, 2016). Hannon and Vereen (2016) speak to irreducibility in counseling by stressing that counselors must be able to "see black men in the context of their ecological world and experiences" (p. 242). The humanistic concept of irreducibility emphasizes "holism and authentic relational encounters as the route to human connection and healing" (Hansen et al., 2014, p. 174). The development of cultural competence, however, is an ever-changing and lifelong process (Ratts et al., 2016), requiring a commitment to cultural humility (ongoing self-critique, self-reflection, collaboration and listening non-judgmentally; Hook et al., 2016). Practicing cultural humility, as a means of side-stepping the reduction of Black and Brown youth to stereotypical versions of themselves, is also valuable in combating cultural appropriation.

Cultural Appropriation

While definitions are vast, Rogers (2006) in part defines cultural appropriation as exploitation stemming from "the use of elements of a subordinated culture by a dominant culture without substantive reciprocity, permission, and/or compensation" (p. 477). Matthes (2019) builds on this position stating that cultural appropriation is wrongful when "it interacts with the oppression of certain cultural group members" (p. 1005), or when it leads to groups being further exploited and marginalized. An important idea in the literature is that cultural appropriation and exploitation are synonymous with colonialism (Todd, 1990). Thinking back on Emdin's (2016) framework for urban youth who identify with hip-hop culture, educators are urged to pinpoint colonial systems of oppression that negatively impact the lives of Black and Brown youth. In the same way that indigenous populations' knowledge and histories have been labeled as primitive and subsequently threatened with erasure through colonial processes (Smith, 2012), the commodification of hip-hop culture is rooted in the labeling of hip-hop as anti-intellectual thus enabling the reduction of its complexities.

Researchers in media literacy laud valid critiques of the commercialization of hip-hop, whose cooperate architects are cultural outsiders, as a process that paints an unjustly narrow and stereotypical perception of both the culture, as well as Black and Latinx youth, akin to cultural exploitation (Reyna et al., 2009). As hip-hop has become more a global phenomenon, the public's (particularly cultural outsiders) understanding of the robustness of hip-hop culture has lessened, and the perceptions of hip-hop as violent, misogynistic and dangerous have hardened (Rose, 2008). There is perhaps no more oppressive process that can be done on to hip-hop culture, and the youth who identify with it, than to snuffle the knowledge of its ability to empower youth and promote resilience in the face of adversity (Travis & Bowman, 2012); to spur innovations in the fields of science, math and technology (Adjapong, 2017; Tillman, 2016); to be woven into curriculum that supports the development of reading and writing literacy (Belle, 2016; Kelly, 2016; Meacham et al., 2019), financial literacy (Burt, 2020), as well as a well-being (Crooke et al., 2020). School counselors, or other educators, attempting to use hip-hop-based practices without the skills to understand the complexities of hip-hop risk engaging the very oppressive and colonial practices Emdin (2016) names as determinantal to Black and Brown youth.

Appropriation in Hip-hop Education

Problems of exploitation at the commercial/societal level trickle down to poor hip-hop practices in education. Given the prominence of hip-hop culture and growth of research and theory on hip-hop-based practices in schools (Cummings et al., 2019; Taylor et al., 2017), it is reasonable to assume that more educators are willing to attempt using hip-hop practices today than they were a decade ago. The goal of this text, unquestionably, is to provide conceptual and empirical support to those who wish to utilize hip-hop practices in their work. In light of this, there are a few important ideas to consider. Roughly 80% of the teaching workforce are White (NCES, 2019), as are 70% of the school counseling workforce (Data USA, 2017), meaning that the majority of do not have a personal, experiential, understanding of the oppressive systems that Black and Brown youth endure. Attempts to use this hip-hop culture in practice, as members of a country and education system that privileges and upholds Whiteness to the extent that White people lack an in-depth understanding of the lived experiences of Black and Brown people (Love, 2019), can be considered cultural appropriation if they are unaware of their ability reenact oppressive practices. According to Matthes (2019), "it is possible for a cultural outsider (even a self-identified one) to avoid wrongful cultural appropriation by working to prevent their actions from manifesting or exacerbating the oppression of cultural insiders" (p. 1007). In this sense, it is the responsibility of educators to develop cultural humility (with regard to hip-hop culture and the Black and Brown experience generally) to develop the requisite skills to prevent their use of hip-hop-based practices from exploiting and oppressing the youth they work with.

Gosa and Fields (2012) offer words of support to those considering deploying hip-hop-based practices, noting that "responsible hip-hop educators should at least be aware that the use of hip-hop by institutions, especially those efforts directed by White people, may activate a long history of distrust" (Gosa & Fields, 2012, p. 187). This research encourages school counselors to, at the very least, consider their purpose in using hip-hop-based approaches in education. Hip-hop school counselors need to assess whether they are using hip-hop practices to validate the goals of the institution or youth-centered outcomes. This cautioning is warranted given the common critique, from members within the hip-hop community, that hip-hop-based practices can utilize a falsely narrow perception of the capabilities of Black and Brown youth (Alim, 2011; Manzano Boulton & Davis 2019).

Alim (2011) critiques traditional language and literacy instruction which operates from the perspective that youth who identify with hip-hop culture are illiterate and require significant support to bolster their grammatical skills. In response, Alim (2011) introduces the concept of ill-literate, suggesting that the "ill in ill-literacies refers not to a 'lack of literacy' but to the presence of skilled literacies" (p. 122). The colonialization of educational systems argument historically draws from the presumption that youth of color lack skills (such as literacy) that can be provided to them by the education system which not only teaches them to be "literate" but also erases the factors that make them "illiterate" (which in most cases has been erroneously named their cultural background; Smith, 2012). Many hip-hop practices, even if well-intentioned, operate in this same capacity. As Alim (2011) pointed out, some educational interventions use hip-hop as a medium to support youth in dropping their skilled literacies to grasp dominant forms of literacy. For example, the use of hip-hop-based web videos of teachers reciting raps to help youth memorize math formulas, or vocabulary words and definitions to increase vocabulary, veer in the direction of using something that is culturally authentic as a medium to, as Gosa and Fields (2012) note, satisfy the goals of the institution. In this sense, if hip-hop-based practices operate from a lens of helping youth highlight illiteracies that need to be fixed, then hip-hop culture is exploited/appropriated as an oppressive and colonial practice that erases cultural knowledge and replaces it with a dominant form of intellect.

While there might be value in learning dominant forms of literacy or memorizing math formulas, Hill and Petchauer (2013) caution educators in their use of hip-hop practices without a nuanced understanding of hip-hop aesthetics and how students' lived experiences can be connected to specific content areas. For example, Emdin et al. (2016) found that the science genius curriculum was effective in having youth write rhymes about the way science interacts with their daily lives, as a means of both mastering academic content and processing emotional stressors. Unfortunately, many hip-hop educators who use hip-hop practices are unable to actively use it as a culturally relevant practice (Irby et al., 2013), and therefore misuse it as a stereotypically informed, trendy engagement practice that risks appropriation.

Therefore, the goal of school counselors looking to be hip-hop educators is to practice cultural humility in effort to resist cultural appropriation, and work toward developing real relationships with youth. The establishment of a strong or real relationship is grounded in authenticity (Gelso, 2009), which young people of color report is missing in their counseling relationships (Lindsey et al., 2013). Humanistic counselors and those seeking to develop cultural humility agree, at least, on one thing: it is necessary to understand the cultural values, beliefs and practices of the people we work with to adequately use culturally relevant approaches. To this end, a detailed understanding of hip-hop culture is essential in learning how to create the conditions for counselors and clients to exist authentically within sessions.

Real Recognize Real

To develop strong therapeutic relationships, in order to deploy HHSWT in response to inauthenticity that youth of color feel, it is necessary to understand how hip-hop culture defines authenticity. Much like Rogers (1961), hip-hop culture also emphasizes the importance of realness (McLeod, 1999). For hip-hop culture, authenticity is a socially agreed upon construct used to combat the threat of assimilation (McLeod, 1999), which school counselors and youth are partnered in combating (Emdin, 2016). As a culture with growing popularity and prominence (Chang, 2005), hip-hop constantly fights to protect its roots (Rose, 2008). Hip-hop emerged out of an urge to speak back against social conditions which oppressed mostly Black and urban communities (Chang, 2005), making it an expectation that participants in the culture use their art as a platform to comment on social issues, circumstances or particular urban beliefs and worldviews (Hill, 2009; Forman, 2002), and protect the erasure of their cultural complexities (McLeod, 1999).

Authenticity in hip-hop is defined in six semantic dimensions which "draw upon [hip-hop] culture's most important symbols in ways that attempt to preserve its identity" (McLeod, 1999, p. 145). Specifically, McLeod (1999) defines the six dimensions of authenticity as: 1) social-psychological, 2) racial, 3) political-economic, 4) social-locational, 5) gender-sexual and 6) cultural. Building on a conceptual HHSWT article on authenticity, which I published in the *Journal of Humanistic Counseling* (Levy, 2020), in this section I further explore these definitions of hip-hop authenticity to assist counselors in a) identifying cultural values which illuminate why youth perceive a lack of authenticity in the counseling relationship and b) using hip-hop-based practices that support counselors in developing cultural humility and supporting authenticity.

Social-Psychological and Racial

Social-psychological debates regarding authenticity in hip-hop culture seek to determine whether or not someone is being true to themselves, or willingly abandoning their own sense of self in pursuit of mass trends. Being able to use your voice to speak to the lived experiences of both yourself and your peers provides novice artists with street credibility, or in this case authenticity (Forman, 2002, McLeod, 1999). Humanists posit that the counseling relationship is threatened when students feel disconnected from their counselor (Lemberger-Truelove & Bowers, 2018), which is evident in the reports of Black and Brown youth feeling unable to relate to their counselors (Lindsey & Marcell, 2012).

The racial authenticity domain pertains to an individual's commitment to speaking to the black experience (McLeod, 1999). As earlier in this text, traditional approaches to counseling lack cultural sensitivity (Tao et al., 2015), and culturally inadequate counseling methodologies both prohibit authentic expression from marginalized populations and lead to a disbelief in the value of counseling (Alvidrez et al., 2008; Earl et al., 2011). It is imperative then that counselors are able to understand the complex realities of Black and Latinx youth to create a space of authentic expression of lived experience (Hannon & Vereen, 2016) and promote racial authenticity (McLeod, 1999). In sum, a solution to social-psychological and racial authenticity violations is two-fold: 1) students must both be able to express themselves, and their experiences with oppression, authentically and 2) students must feel that their counselor can fully digest what they are expressing.

Authenticity Intervention

To support students in expressing themselves, and their experiences with oppression, authentically, counseling interventions must offer youth the opportunity to feel heard, validated and unjudged by their clinician. School counselors must be able to use interventions that resonate with youth emotionally (Hansen, 2005) and enable authentic introspection (McWilliams, 2005). To offer youth a counseling process that is aligned with both social-psychological and racial authenticity, I proposed that hip-hop lyric writing could be used by counselors to "encourage youth to construct introspective lyrics supporting exploration of their lived experiences and particular emotional themes covered in sessions" (Levy, 2020, p. 44). As an intervention, hip-hop lyric writing is supported by research indicating that counselors who use hip-hop-based interventions have been perceived by clients as more relatable (Kobin & Tyson, 2006), and that Black and Latinx youth report more comfort evoking thought and feelings through lyric writing than traditional talk therapy (Gonzalez & Hayes, 2009; Levy & Keum, 2014).

School Counselor's Cultural Humility Practice

School counselors who attempt to use hip-hop lyric writing as an intervention, however, must be aware of the tensions surrounding cultural appropriation; that is, how can hip-hop lyric writing be used without exploiting youth and enacting oppressive practices? For example, as a practicing school counselor at a Charter high school, I was often asked by my principal to bring students up to her office to perform some of their emotionally themed raps for the current and potential school donors. While this practice was exciting for the students (because they enjoyed performing), it disproportionately benefited the school (validating the goals of the institution) at the risk of exploiting students' vulnerable thoughts and feelings for monetary gain. I recall my principal asking me, sincerely, "do you think they'll become famous rappers?", reinforcing a reductionistic perception of both youth who identify with hip-hop and capacity for hip-hop to be used as a healing practice.

To adequately utilize lyric writing as an intervention, school counselors need to be able to actively listen to hip-hop lyrics for the holistic representation of youths' lived experiences. It is recommended that school counselors wishing to use this practice spend considerable time analyzing hip-hop lyrics for the same expressed cognitive and affective content beyond their own biases. By finding hip-hop lyrics to analyze, counselors can self-reflect on their own biases toward youth culture (practice cultural humility), as well as prepare to engage with students in a capacity that supports empathic connection and unconditional positive regard. Practically, I recommend counselors print out hip-hop lyrics and use highlighters to pinpoint emotional and cognitive statements that can be discussed in session with youth. Additionally, counselors should be willing to begin this work by asking youth to share songs, music videos or lyrics that resonate with them. Levy (2020) found that school counselors who analyzed hip-hop lyrics and music videos for emotional and cognitive themes reported a better understanding of their active listening skills, as well as the ability to pinpoint deficits in their counseling practice. Lastly, based on the presumption that youth want to display social-psychological and racial authenticity, counselors can inquire about the meaning behind the lyrics students write, and even push students to consider re-writing rhymes to more accurately reflect their thoughts and feelings.

It is only when counselors have done the necessary cultural humility work they facilitate the students writing of their own content, and then utilize active listening skills to effectively process, discuss and validate the thoughts and feelings presented in the hip-hop lyrics they bring to session. Through the practice of cultural humility and use of hip-hop lyric writing interventions in session, counseling professionals can seek empathetic understanding as they foster excitement among youth to pen lyrics that accurately speak to their real, Black and Brown, experience. The lyric writing process encourages youth to bring their genuine selves and experiences into session and explore an identity that transcends the reductionistic perspective the complexities of hip-hop culture. Youth can engage in this social-psychological and racial authenticity practice in session because they interact with a counselor who has done the self-work needed to exist authentically and to be perceived authentically.

Political-Economic and Social-Locational Dimensions

McLeod (1999) further outlines the political-economic and the social-locational dimensions of authenticity concerning the concept of selling out. When considering political-economic authenticity, selling out is a deliberate removal of one's genuine persona and music from the streets or underground (the hip-hop-based community from which they came), to enter a music business culture and embrace a commercial success (McLeod, 1999). Similarly, the social-locational dimensions of authenticity compare the streets with the suburbs, positing that an individual's remove of self, physically, from the streets or hood to live in a more affluent area are suggests they are "distancing themselves from their roots" (p. 143) and therefore inauthentic. Therefore, notions of "staying independent" are of great importance in the maintenance of political-economic authenticity. Independence in this hip-hop capacity represents a student's sense of alignment with their own personal network of resources (intrapersonal and interpersonal). The social-locational component of authenticity "keepin' it real means not disassociating oneself from the community from which one came – the street" (McLeod, 1999, p. 142). The counseling field has been ridiculed for selling out on core humanistic traditions (empathic connection, congruence or unconditional positive), allowing counselors to lose sight of relationship building while trying to deploy practical interventions (Hansen et al., 2014). Discourse around Hip-hop practices in education has similarly cautioned the use of interventions that operate from a stereotypical and or narrow cultural lens (Gosa & Fields, 2012). Solutions must be hip-hop-based interventions that are rooted in both humanistic principles and a robust understanding of hip-hop culture.

Authenticity Intervention

Humanistic counselors work toward validating their student's contextual experiences because they know that without the relational aspect of the counseling process, they will "decontextualize the [the student] from his/her environment" (Cosgrove & McHugh, 2000, p. 824). The humanistic perspective prioritizes supporting student's development through understanding how social, cultural and political factors converge to impact their psychological growth or congruence in their self-concept (Hansen et al., 2014). Interventions that address a variety of contextual factors must be rooted in knowledge regarding how students culturally address their emotional challenges (Laska et al., 2014). If counselors use interventions that fail to recognize the knowledge's, beliefs and worldviews of hip-hop culture, students will be forced to sell out on their genuine persona and personal resources in order to heal. In contrast, a humanistic school counselor should operate from the belief that the clients hold the ability to generate their own solutions (Hansen et al., 2014). To support the political-economic and social-locational domains of authenticity in hip-hop, counselors must support and validate clients in pulling from their personal network of resources, and staying true to their roots, as they work toward addressing their present concerns.

The process of creating hip-hop mixtapes supports youth in identifying an emotional theme of importance to them, and then researching, writing and recording a collection of songs about that theme. Aiding students in the mixtape creation process, counselors encourage youth to go beyond online research on their emotional theme and analyze their personal experiences as well as information available to them within their interpersonal network. For example, students might reach out to their family or community to find hip-hop beats or recording equipment to support their writing and recording of emotionally themed lyrics. Students might also schedule interviews with their friends, family and community members about a given emotional theme to support the exploration of their own thoughts, feelings and creation of lyrics. Through mixtape creation "counselors validate clients' desire to maintain independence by supporting them in tapping their personal network to aid them in the helping process and stay true to their cultural beliefs around healing and emotional challenges" (Levy, 2020, p. 48). The belief that the clients are in possession of all the faculties necessary to solve their own problems is inherently humanistic and promoted via the hip-hop mixtape intervention.

School Counselor's Cultural Humility Practice

Preparation for mixtape making work with youth requires that counselors trust in youth's ability to tap into their intrapersonal and interpersonal network of resources as a part of the healing process. Ultimately, this requires that counselors develop a nuanced understanding of the hip-hop community. Prospective hip-hop school counselors should begin deepening their understanding of hip-hop culture by reading about the history of hip-hop. Jeff Chang's (2005) *Can't Stop Won't Stop Can't Stop Won't Stop: A History of the Hip-Hop Generation* highlights the beauty and resilience of the hip-hop community to corral around one another to push back against a variety of systemic inequities. A variety of hip-hop documentaries, art exhibits and entire museums also exist and can be explored to deepen one's awareness. Practical demonstrations of the supportive nature of the hip-hop community can also be directly experienced by school counselors who are willing to travel to local open mic nights or local park cyphers. By attending hip-hop community events, those who may only see hip-hop through a stereotypical lens are offered an experiential opportunity to witness values, beliefs and knowledge the community practices.

For example, one of the most transformative moments I have had, as a school counselor and scholar, was at an open mic night. In 2017, I moved to Boston, Massachusetts, where I did not know anyone within the hip-hop community. Looking to tap into the hip-hop community, I attended an open mic night to perform some songs. As I stared into the audience, fear rushed forward with the realization that it had been months since my last performance, and I had forgotten all the lyrics. A fight or flight response kicked in and, upon noticing this, the host for the evening told the DJ to turn the beat off, put his arm around me and said "You're dope, and we want to hear your words. Don't worry about messing up here". The DJ proceeded to turn the beat back on, and the crowd chanted "run it back, run it back!", indicating that they would like to hear me start the song over. I collected myself and performed the song with no mistakes. This experience exemplified the power and potential of hip-hop culture, to corral around others and to support cultural participants through difficult and vulnerable experiences. In a moment that I felt like I had personally lost control and wanted to give up, the community carried me.

My experience attending an open mic nights have hardened the personal belief that within hip-hop spaces it was both ok to be vulnerable and imperative that participants trust the community will support them unconditionally so long as they present themselves authentically. Attending hip-hop community events can similarly offer others experiential learning opportunities. The use of the mixtape in the counseling process, and the belief that youth can find members within their community to support the creation of the mixtape, stems from experiential knowledge regarding the values and beliefs of the hip-hop community. Beyond reading about hip-hop culture and the importance of community (and watching documentaries about the same), I urge future hip-hop school counselors to research and attend hip-hop events to experience and witness its cultural complexities firsthand.

Gender-Sexual Dimension

The gender-sexual dimensions of authenticity criticize being emotional, suggesting that demonstrations of weakness or vulnerability make one "soft" or fake. These claims support being "hard" (able to push-through challenges) as a symbol of being real (McLeod, 1999). The gender-sexual aspect of hip-hop's authenticity demonstrates the importance of clients' belief in themselves to address concerns independently, and for counselors to support that process. Humanistic counselors create empathic and judgment-free spaces for clients to bring their true selves to session and use active listening skills to support the exploration of knowledge/answers within the client to support the belief in their own ability to persevere (Rogers, 1961).

Authenticity Intervention

Countering barriers to emotional expression is essential in humanistic practice, mostly in the establishment of warm and accepting environments that invite emotional disclosure. The use of hip-hop cyphers, "highly codi-fied yet unstructured practices where youth who identify with hip-hop cul-ture information exchange in the form of raps or dance", has been explored in group counseling practice to establish group norms support-ive of group cohesion. Scholars have argued that using hip-hop cyphers in group counseling enables clients to enact a series of predefined norms and/or rules of engagement that support emotional expression. Considering the gender-sexual dimension of hip-hop authenticity further, there is a specific distinction between being perceived as hard (distanced from emotions as a means to appear in control), and soft (being perceived as weak or vulnerable), with soft being a marker of inauthenticity (McLeod, 1999). Expression of emotions through hip-hop lyric writing is discussed as a socially and culturally acceptable tool that enables clients to express emotions while side-stepping vulnerability and weakness (Levy & Keum, 2014); that is, counselors who use hip-hop-based interventions, like shar-ing lyrics in group cyphers, enable a socially acceptable context for clients to feel vulnerable as they open up to others, while being personally empowered to believe in their ability to find answers to their own problems.

School Counselor's Cultural Humility Practice

As a cultural humility practice, school counselors hold the responsibility of creating pipelines to hip-hop cultural events that all students are invited to participate in. School counselors are expected to develop part-nerships within the community to support student development (Bryan et al., 2019). I have also recommended that school counselors attend community events to gather experience about hip-hop culture. Once relationships have been built within the community, the school coun-selor can establish partnerships with community members to offer youth a chance to perform either local open mic nights or hip-hop cyphers. School counselors might even create their own open mic nights at their school, inviting community members to host them. Conversely, through discussions with students, counselors might find that there are parents within the community who engage with hip-hop. This too, would provide a chance to invite parents to host events or workshops for youth. This public type of sharing within hip-hop spaces is what scholars have argued offers clients a socially acceptable platform to disclose difficult thoughts and feelings. Ultimately, these practices require that the counselor rec-ognize their ability to support students in tapping into their own cultural forms of healing as a means to engage in the counseling process. Counselors must be ready to admit that they themselves do not have the answers to the students' concerns, or the resources to support students through healing, but they can play an important role in helping their students become aware of their internal and interpersonal resources.

Through these techniques, counselors practice humility, and the clients and their community can prosper as they are able to utilize their own knowledge, values and beliefs as healing.

Cultural Dimension

Finally, the cultural dimension "addresses hip-hop' status as a culture that has deep resonating traditions, rather than as a commodity" (McLeod, 1999, p. 143). This dimension directly aligns with the humanistic principle of irreducibility, which calls for counselors to view students at complex individuals and avoid reducing them to stereotypes, objects or phenomena (Hannon & Vereen, 2016). For hip-hop culture, the threat of reduction has always existed. Hip-hop was born out of a need to promote Black and Latinx voice that was being stifled systemically (Chang, 2005). Today, many educators who intend to deploy hip-hop-based practice operate from a reductionistic perspective that limits the opportunity of youth to showcase their skills and potential beyond the stereotypical confines of the practitioner's lens (Gosa & Fields, 2012; Irby et al., 2013). For hip-hop culture, the definition of cultural authenticity requires treating one's voice as a holistic representation of their experience, as opposed to reducing it to a product. The lesson for school counselors is to practice cultural humility, to ensure they are committed to irreducibility while using hip-hop-based interventions.

Authenticity Intervention

Each of the aforementioned hip-hop tools for counselors identifies salient cultural practices that the hip-hop community engages in (the cypher, the mixtape, lyric writing and collaboration, as well as locating hip-hop event spaces). It is argued that the use of these practices by school counselors enables students to feel heard and valued as holding answers to their own concerns. By leaning on interventions that help students use their cultural forms of healing and catharsis to guide the session, counselors support students in bringing their genuine and whole selves into session (Levy, 2019). In this sense, hip-hops authenticity and irreducibility are in line with each other. As per Kobin and Tyson (2006), counselors who use hip-hop approaches in counseling sessions are perceived positively by students, as people they can connect with.

School Counselor's Cultural Humility Practice

In effort to deepen one's awareness of hip-hop as a culture, beyond attending events, watching documentaries and reading articles, it is recommended that school counselors establish routines to stay tapped into developments in hip-hop culture. One of the most notable qualities of hip-hop is how it has developed overtime, which is also a challenge for those who wish to use it in practice with relevance. I have heard many hip-hop educators talk about how they are using classic Tupac and Notorious B.I.G. songs in class, who have not been particularly relevant to youth for quite some time. While the history of hip-hop can be addressed in the school counselors' work, it is more important that we create opportunities for youth to share with us their versions of hip-hop. Youth lead and create new iterations of the culture, and we must do our due diligence to understand and validate those innovations. If we truly aim to operate from a perspective of unconditional positive regard, then we cannot believe that versions of hip-hop that we might know are superior to newer versions of hip-hop that youth engage with. A commitment to staying attuned to developments in hip-hop requires that school counselors trust youth to enlighten them. Once counselors build these connections with youth, then they may expose them to older versions of hip-hop for which they might not be privy. In addition to asking youth to share about developments in hip-hop, school counselors can stay on top of new hip-hop events that enter the community, as well as following Apple Music or Spotify playlists up and coming artists. Via social outlets like Instagram, school counselors can follow their local hip-hop radio stations (i.e., Hot97 in New York City) and national hip-hop news outlets like Complex.

Conclusion

In this chapter, substantial consideration was given to the establishment of relationships with youth amidst deploying HHSWT. Additionally, hip-hop education practices were reviewed to interrogate how outsiders to hip-hop culture might use hip-hop interventions and wrongfully appropriate. HHSWT is rooted in humanistic counseling principles, as well as cultural practices of hip-hop, which both value promoting authenticity to explore a robust self-concept. This chapter reviewed how both humanistic counselors and the hip-hop community define authenticity, and appropriation, to pinpoint discrepancies in counselors' practices that might explain why Black and Latinx youth feel disconnected. As a solution, a series of strategies were explored for school counselors to develop authentic relationships with youth and engage in cultural humility practices to resist appropriation and embrace authenticity.

References

Adjapong, E. S. (2017). Bridging theory and practice in the urban science classroom: A framework for hip-hop pedagogy in STEM. *Critical Education, 8*(15), 5–23. http://ojs.library.ubc.ca/index.php/criticaled/article/view/186248

Alim, H. S. (2011). Global ill-literacies: Hip hop cultures, youth identities, and the politics of literacy. *Review of Research in Education, 35*(1), 120–146. DOI: 10.3102/0091732X10383208

Alvidrez, J., Snowden, L. R., & Kaiser, D. M. (2008). The experience of stigma among Black mental health consumers. *Journal of Health Care for the Poor and Underserved, 19*(3), 874–893. doi:10.1353/hpu.0.0058

Aubrey, R. F. (1977). Historical development of guidance and counseling and implications for the future. *Personnel & Guidance Journal, 55*(6), 288–295. https://doi.org/10.1002/j.2164-4918.1977.tb04991.x

Belle, C. (2016). Don't believe the hype: Hip-hop literacies and English education. *Journal of Adolescent & Adult Literacy, 60*(3), 287–294.

Bryan, J., Griffin, D., Kim, J., Griffin, D. M., & Young, A. (2019). school counselor leadership in school-family-community partnerships: An equity-focused partnership process model for moving the field forward. In Sheldon, S.B., & Turner-Vorbeck, T.A. (Eds.) *The Wiley handbook on family, school, and community relationships in education*, 265–287. John Wiley & Sons.

Burt, I. (2020). I get money: A therapeutic financial literacy group for black teenagers. *The Journal for Specialists in Group Work, 45*(2), 165–181. https://doi.org/10.1080/01933922.2020.1740845

Crooke, A. H. D., Comte, R., & Almeida, C. M. (2020). Hip-hop as an agent for health and wellbeing in schools. *Voices: A World Forum for Music Therapy. 20*(1), 1–24. https://doi.org/10.15845/voices.v20i1.2870

Chang, J. (2005). *Can't stop won't stop: A history of the hip-hop generation.* New York: St Martin's Press.

Cosgrove, L., & McHugh, M. C. (2000). Speaking for ourselves: Feminist methods and community psychology. *American Journal of Community Psychology, 28*(6), 815–838. doi:10.1023/A:1005163817007

Cummings, R., Chambers, B., Reid, A., & Gosha, K. (2019). *STEM hip-hop pedagogy: A meta-synthesis on hip-hop pedagogy STEM interventions tools for underrepresented minorities in K-12 education.* In *Proceedings of the 2019 ACM Southeast Conference, Kennesaw State University, Kennesaw, GA* (pp. 46–52).

Data USA (2017). Counselors by race/ethnicity. Retrieved from https://datausa.io/profile/soc/counselors#demographics

Earl, T., Williams, D., & Anglade, S. (2011). An update on the mental health of black Americans: Puzzling dilemmas and needed research. *Journal of Black Psychology, 37*(4), 485–498. doi:10.1177/0095798410396077

Emdin, C. (2010). Affiliation and alienation: Hip-hop, rap, and urban science education. *Journal of Curriculum Studies, 42*(1), 1–25. doi:10.1080/00220270903161118

Emdin, C. (2016). *For white folks who teach in the hood… and the rest of y'all too: Reality pedagogy and urban education.* Beacon Press.

Emdin, C., Adjapong, E., & Levy, I. (2016). Hip-hop based interventions as pedagogy/therapy in STEM: A model from urban science education. *Journal for Multicultural Education, 10*(1), 307–321. doi: 10.1108/JME-03-2016-0023

Forman, M. (2002). *The 'hood comes first: Race, space, and place in rap and hip-hop.* CT: Wesleyan.

Gelso, C. J. (2009). The time has come: The real relationship in psychotherapy research. *Psychotherapy Research, 19*(3), 278–282.

Gonzalez, T., & Hayes, B. G. (2009). Rap music in school counseling based on Don Elligan's rap therapy. *Journal of Creativity in Mental Health, 4*(2), 161–172. doi:10.1080/15401380902945293

Gosa, T. L., & Fields, T. G. (2012). Is hip-hop education another hustle. In Portfilio, B.J. & Viola, M.J. (Eds.) *The (Ir) responsible use of Hip-hop as pedagogy,* 181–196. Peter Lang.

Hannon, M. D., & Vereen, L. G. (2016). Irreducibility of black male clients: Considerations for culturally competent counseling. doi:10.1002/johc.12036

Hansen, J. T. (2005). Postmodernism and humanism: A proposed integration of perspectives that value human meaning systems. *The Journal of Humanistic Counseling, Education and Development, 44,* 3–15. doi:10.1002/j.2164-490X.2005. tb00052.x

Hansen, J. T., Speciale, M., & Lemberger, M. E. (2014). Humanism: The foundation and future of professional counseling. *Journal of Humanistic Counseling, 53*(3), 170–190. doi:10.1002/j.2161-1939.2014.00055.x

Hill, M. L. (2009). *Beats, rhymes, and classroom life: Hip-hop pedagogy and the politics of identity.* Teachers College Press.

Hill, M. L., & Petchauer, E. (2013). *Schooling hip-hop: Expanding hip-hop based education across the curriculum.* Teachers College Press.

Hook, J. N., Farrell, J. E., Davis, D. E., DeBlaere, C., Van Tongeren, D. R., & Utsey, S. O. (2016). Cultural humility and racial microaggressions in counseling. *Journal of Counseling Psychology, 63*(3), 269–277. doi:10.1037/cou0000114

Irby, D. J., Hall, H. B., & Hill, M. L. (2013). Schooling teachers, schooling ourselves: Insights and reflections from teaching K-12 teachers how to use hip-hop to educate students. *International Journal of Multicultural Education, 15*(1), 1–18. https://ijme-journal.org/index.php/ijme/article/viewFile/527/825.

Kelly, L. L. (2016). "You don't have to claim her" reconstructing black femininity through critical hip-hop literacy. *Journal of Adolescent & Adult Literacy, 59*(5), 529–538.

Kobin, C., & Tyson, E. (2006). Thematic analysis of hip-hop music: Can hip-hop in therapy facilitate empathic connections when working with clients in urban settings? *The Arts in Psychotherapy, 33*(4), 343–356. doi:10.1016/j.aip.2006.05.001

Kruse, A. J. (2016). Being hip-hop: Beyond skills and songs. *General Music Today, 30*(1), 53–58. doi:10.1177/1048371316658931

LaMantia, K., Wagner, H., & Bohecker, L. (2015). Ally development through feminist pedagogy: A systemic focus on intersectionality. *Journal of LGBT Issues in Counseling, 9*(2), 136–153. doi:10.1080/15538605.2015.1029205

Laska, K. M., Gurman, A. S., & Wampold, B. E. (2014). Expanding the lens of evidence-based practice in psychotherapy: A common factors perspective. *Psychotherapy, 51*(4), 467.

Lemberger-Truelove, M. E., & Bowers, H. (2018). An advocating student-within-environment approach to school counseling. In Dollarhide, C.T., & Lemberger-Truelove, M.E. (Eds.) *Theories of school counseling for the 21st century* (pp. 266–294). Oxford University Press.

Levy, I. (2019). Hip-hop and spoken word therapy in urban school counseling. *Professional School Counseling, 22*(1b).

Levy, I. (2020). "Real recognize real": Hip-hop spoken word therapy and humanistic practice. *The Journal of Humanistic Counseling, 59*(1), 38–53. doi:10.1002/johc.12128

Levy, I., & Keum, B. T. (2014). Hip-hop emotional exploration in men. *Journal of Poetry Therapy, 27*(4), 217–223. doi:10.1080/08893675.2014.949528

Lindsey, M. A., Chambers, K., Pohle, C., Beall, P., & Lucksted, A. (2013). Understanding the behavioral determinants of mental health service use by urban, under-resourced black youth: Adolescent and caregiver perspectives. *Journal of Child and Family Studies, 22*(1), 107–121. doi:10.1007/s10826-012-9668-z

Lindsey, M. A., & Marcell, A. V. (2012). "We're going through a lot of struggles that people don't even know about": The need to understand African American males' help-seeking for mental health on multiple levels. *American Journal of Men's Health, 6*(5), 354–364. doi:10.1177/1557988312441520

Love, B. (2019). *We want to do more than survive: Abolitionist teaching and the pursuit of educational freedom.* Beacon Press.

Manzano Boulton, E., & Davis, E. (2019). The relationship between empathy and theoretical orientation of counselors-in-training. *The Journal of Counselor Preparation and Supervision, 12*(4), 5.

McLeod, K. (1999). Authenticity within hip-hop and other cultures threatened with assimilation. *Journal of Communication, 49*(4), 134–150. doi:10.1111/j.1460-2466.1999.tb02821.x

McWilliams, N. (2005). Preserving our humanity as therapists. *Psychotherapy: Theory, Research, Practice, Training, 42*(2), 139–151. doi:10.1037/0033-3204.42.2.139

Meacham, S. J., Meacham, S., Thompson, M., & Graves, H. (2019). Hip-hop early literacy in K–1 classrooms. *The Reading Teacher, 73*(1), 29–37.

Matthes, E.H. (2019) Cultural appropriation and oppression. *Philosophical Studies, 176*, 1003–1013. https://doi.org/10.1007/s11098-018-1224-2

National Center for Education Statistics (2019). Characteristics of public school teachers by race/ethnicity. Retrieved from https://nces.ed.gov/programs/raceindicators/spotlight_a.asp

Neal, M. A. (2012). No time for fake Niggas: Hip-hop culture and the authenticity debates. *That's the Joint!: The Hip-hop Studies Reader, 2*, 69–71.

Ratts, M. J., Singh, A. A., Nassar-McMillan, S., Butler, S. K., & McCullough, J. R. (2016). Multicultural and social justice counseling competencies: Guidelines for the counseling profession. *Journal of Multicultural Counseling and Development, 44*(1), 28–48. doi:10.1002/jmcd.12035

Reyna, C., Brandt, M., & Viki, G. T. (2009). Blame it on hip-hop: Anti-rap attitudes as a proxy for prejudice. *Group Processes & Intergroup Relations, 12*(3), 361–380. doi:10.1177/1368430209102848

Rose, T. (2008). *The hip-hop wars: What we talk about when we talk about hip-hop—and why it matters.* Civitas Books.

Rogers, R. A. (2006). From cultural exchange to transculturation: A review and reconceptualization of cultural appropriation. *Communication Theory, 16*(4), 474-503. https://doi.org/10.1111/j.1468-2885.2006.00277.x

Rogers, C. R. (1957). The necessary and sufficient conditions of therapeutic personality change. *Journal of Counseling Psychology, 21*(2), 9.

Rogers, C. R. (1961). The characteristics of a helping relationship. In *On becoming a person* (pp. 39–58).

Smith, L. T. (2012). *Decolonizing methodologies: Research and indigenous peoples.* Zed Books.

Tao, K. W., Owen, J., Pace, B. T., & Imel, Z. E. (2015). A meta-analysis of multicultural competencies and psychotherapy process and outcome. *Journal of Counseling Psychology, 62*(3), 337–350. doi:10.1037/cou0000086

Taylor, R. D., Oberle, E., Durlak, J. A., & Weissberg, R. P. (2017). Promoting positive youth development through school-based social and emotional learning interventions: A meta-analysis of follow-up effects. *Child Development, 88*(4), 1156–1171.

Teding van Berkhout, E., & Malouff, J. M. (2016). The efficacy of empathy training: A meta-analysis of randomized controlled trials. *Journal of counseling psychology, 63*(1), 32.

Tillman, D. A. (2016). Learning from the college dropout: Depictions of numeracy and mathematics within hip-hop music. *Journal of Mathematics Education, 9*, 53–71.

Todd, L. (1990). Notes on appropriation. *Parallelogramme 16*(1), 24-33.

Travis, R., & Bowman, S. W. (2012). Ethnic identity, self-esteem and variability in perceptions of rap music's empowering and risky influences. *Journal of Youth Studies, 15*(4), 455–478.

Wang, X. (2012). 'I am not a qualified dialect rapper': Constructing hip-hop authenticity in China. *Sociolinguistic Studies, 6*(2), 333.

Watkins, D. C., Walker, R. L., & Griffith, D. M. (2010). A meta-study of black male mental health and well-being. *Journal of Black Psychology, 36*(3), 303–330. doi:10.1177/0095798409353756

4 Co-Creating Counseling Offices with Youth

Co-Creating Counseling Offices with Youth

Moving from the use of HHSWT to bolster intra- and interpersonal dynamics in the counseling relationship, I also wanted to consider if the physical environment where the HHSWT took place could impact outcomes. When first beginning to deploy HHSWT as a school counselor, I placed a microphone in the corner of my office with the aim of drawing students into counseling. I believed it would be quite effective to transition from talking about a particular emotional theme in a counseling session, to writing lyrics and recording a song. After a number of group sessions, where discussion, writing and recording took place, one student mentioned, "You know, this isn't really a studio". The group agreed and went on to explain that they wanted particular decor (posters, a couch, a lamp, etc.) and a studio equipment (a second computer, a beat machine, more headphones, etc.) that was currently missing within the space. This discussion culminated in the group co-developing a campaign on DonorsChoose (a website for educators to request financial support for projects with students) in an attempt to crowd-source funding for a studio space, which resulted in $1,000 in donations. With new decor and equipment, our group work continued, but requests from students to add more to the studio space to make it feel authentic did not subside. Over a total of 3 years, DonorsChoose campaigns generated $3,000 in funding. During this process, students even identified another room within the school building, equipped with a large rectangular window that would become the new studio space. I won't soon forget the excitement on students' faces as we marveled at how much the new office looked like a "real studio", with a recording booth behind the glass window. To finalize the creation of the new studio space, students advocated for support from the custodial staff, who not only helped with drilling, wiring and hanging pictures but also recorded some of their own music with students.

While anecdotally I felt the construction of the hip-hop studio was an important part of the group counseling process, there was no data collected to explore its impact on students or the larger school community. That is, it is hard to imagine that engaging youth in the co-creation of the environment for which they engaged in counseling did not influence the outcome data of the HHSWT pilot study, particularly given the number of school building stakeholders who organically became involved in the work. The experiences I had developed as a school counselor, learning with students as we built a studio, deserved further study with the aim of distilling a counseling environment construction process. In this chapter, I explore data from a follow-up study where I partnered with a school and their youth to construct a school studio as a school counseling office. It should be noted that I do not argue that school counselors need thousands of dollars for a studio to use HHSWT. Instead this chapter speaks to the importance of co-constructing environments with students.

School Counseling Environments

Little is known about the construction of physical school counseling spaces. Existing research on the design of counseling environments explores the offices of mental health counselors or counseling psychologists, in non-school spaces. Additionally, a fair amount of research within the counseling environment field assesses the impact of the counseling environment on the counseling profession, based on the assumption that their well-being impacts their job performance (Rogers et al., 2018). For example, researchers found that counselors who have the ability to customize their offices reported less stress and increased job satisfaction (Préssly & Heesacker, 2001), creativity and perceived well-being (Ceylan et al., 2008), much of which is quite dated.

A singular, and perhaps only, school counseling study found that the creation of calm and comfortable environments supported students with emoting (Cook & Malloy, 2014). Counselor-made changes to their offices appear to have value in well-being outcomes for clients. Aesthetic changes, like dim lighting, or furniture that connote feelings of a home, or lounge, can positively impact the client's perceived stress (Miwa & Hanyu, 2006; Sanders & Lehmann, 2018). Open environments with good sources of natural lighting, which also maintain privacy, are imperative in counseling environment design (Huffcut, 2010). Changes to the layout of a counseling office predict a client's psychological state, specifically, researchers found that counseling environments can support youth in exploring difficult emotions and addressing tensions within their self-concept (Liddicoat, 2015).

Of concern within counseling office design literature, however, is the focus on the choices of counseling professionals instead of considering the client's role in the physical environment design (Goelitz & Stewart-Kahn, 2008). For example, researchers indicated that counselors placed paintings of multicultural art on the walls of their counseling office in an attempt to be perceived as culturally competent (Devlin et al., 2013). These attempts double-down on the already problematic power dynamics in the counseling relationship (i.e., counselor as an expert) by implying that counselors know the client's culture well enough to visually demonstrate competence. In chapter 3 of this book, I reviewed how much of the work required to establish cultural humility is relational, and stems from acknowledging the client as an expert of cultural and experiential knowledge of which the counselor is often unaware. In short, authenticity is felt and established through rapport building, and is not something that we can solve with the placement of a painting. This critique on design, however, should not be directed at individual counselors who choose to place the painting on their walls to demonstrate competence, but on the structural systems of oppression that operate within schools (Emdin, 2016). Namely, we must critique the counseling field who have engaged in minimal research surrounding the construction of culturally appropriate school counseling environments (Benton & Overtree, 2012; Pearson & Wilson, 2012) and have appeared to have only included a single guideline on a multicultural competence checklist, reading, "the physical surroundings of the program area reflect an appreciation of cultural diversity (e.g., artwork, posters, paintings, languages heard)" (Ponterotto & Austin, 2005, p. 31). Guidelines like this place school counselors in a position to select décor they believe will be culturally responsive, which runs counter to what we know about the intersections of HHSWT, humanism and cultural competence (i.e., the students have the answers, we must actively listen to them to inform design).

Classroom Design

In contrast to the school counseling field, the field of teaching has done a bit more exploration of the classroom environment's impact on learning. Mohanan (2002) introduced the design of classroom spaces with the term "built pedagogy", as a way of defining how a teacher's teaching philosophy, values and theoretical orientation manifest toward either discipline or autonomy-centered classrooms. Educators who value autonomy and youth voice will support the creation of open classrooms that can easily adapt to meet student's needs (Monahan, 2002). Specific design choices that teachers make to their classroom spaces can increase or restrict student engagement (Rands & Gansemer-Topf, 2017). Specifically, the creation of a classroom with an open environment (Barber, 2006; Hunley and Schaler, 2006), flexibility in seating arrangement and a variety of writing surfaces (Sanders, 2013), multiple student technologies (Brewe et al., 2012), and bright and natural lighting (Sleegers et al., 2012) can all positively impact teaching and learning. Using single-subject research design at a school in Australia, Imms and Byers (2017) found that student engagement and positive perceptions of the quality of their teachers were improved as a result of the use of one-on-technologies as well as spacious and malleable classroom arrangements. Similarly, Rands and Gansemer-Topf (2017) found that student-centered, open and flexible learning environments increased the prevalence of active learning strategies, where students shared thoughts, feelings, values and utilized higher-order thinking as opposed to rote-memorization. Value of authentic student voice, therefore, transcends the placement of multicultural items on walls. Similar problems exist within teaching, where educators are rightfully criticized for the belief that placing flags of different countries in their classroom is enough to substantiate their cultural competence (Ladson-Billings, 2020).

Cultivating School Culture

Feelings of flexibility, autonomy and cultural relevance are not only important within counseling offices and classrooms but should also be pervasive throughout school culture to support students' academic, career and social/emotional development (Lewis et al., 2016). For example, school counselors work with students, families and teachers in understanding and supporting each student's individualized development (ASCA, 2019). The same can be said for classroom teachers who use cogenerative dialogues to partner with students in constructing a classroom environment supportive of everyone's needs (Emdin, 2010). Educators aiming to engage in work that shapes school culture follow a similar trajectory wherein they establish coordination among all building stakeholders around a shared vision appreciative of cultural difference and inclusivity (Hall & Hord, 2015, Hannigan et al., 2019).

In light of this, educators have partnered with youth for the express activating them as leaders in the school community who collaborate to instill the changes they want (Duckworth et al., 2019). Youth leadership is rooted in the belief that student development should include time focused on solving problems within the world (Siegel, 2013). Youth Participatory Action Research, a process by which youth engage in the research and dissemination of projects that aim to address issues they deem relevant to their lives, can be used as a medium to support youth in advocacy within their school community (Cook et al., 2020). Art therapy approaches are evidenced as useful in supporting an inclusive school culture facilitative of student's well-being (Hannigan et al., 2019). When working with Black and Brown youth, offering culturally responsive approaches to push back against, and ultimately change, oppressive school policies becomes paramount (Emdin, 2016). Scholars have posited that hip-hop allows participants an avenue to become social actors who use art as a way of engaging in advocacy that is connected to their experiences with oppressive systems (Forman, 2013). To support youth in leveraging their voice and experiences to advocate for, equitable, structural changes within their school's community and culture, school counselors play a critical role (Hines et al., 2020). Instead of focusing solely on individual student development, school counselors are charged with understanding how they have perpetuated practices that marginalize Black and Brown youth (Martin, 2015) and with addressing larger systemic concerns in school buildings that impact youth's development (Holcomb-McCoy, 2007).

Hip-Hop Studios

In an effort to create a systemic shift within school counseling programs and school buildings, I urge educators to empower youth to co-construct their own environments within schools, as a direct pivot away from the traditional counseling office design that is devoid of youth input. Drawing from Monahan (2000) "built pedagogy", a culturally sensitive counseling environment must enable flexibility in the school counselors' use of theory, ideals and practices of HHSWT. A core construct of HHSWT is the belief that youth hold the tools to establish authenticity within counseling sessions (Levy, 2020), and therefore construction must enable youth to share their inherent culture knowledge and expertise. This type of school counseling environment creation must first begin with an exploration of a physical space that has held an important place in hip-hop culture, th*e hip-hop recording studio.*

Hip-hop studios are described as symbolic spaces or places "in which identity and meaning are shaped by social exchanges that occur within a culturally specific location" (Harkness, 2014, p. 85). Within studios themselves, artists are afforded the chance to explore thoughts and feelings, as a means of cultivating a strong identity and self-concept, even regarded by Harkness (2014) as "sites for legitimization and personal transformation" (p. 85). In hip-hop culture, home-studios emerged as spaces for artists to control their integrity and engage in their own creation and distribution of content outside of the corporate music milieu (Harkness, 2014). The home-studios hold a unique position in hip-hop because they afford artists' total control over how they present themselves and are often built on low budgets, and wherever they can fit (i.e., closets, basements, living rooms or bathrooms; Harkness, 2014).

A qualitative analysis of rappers and producer's studio construction revealed they preferred environments to be aesthetically pleasing, with foam padding on the walls and dim lighting. Artists stressed the importance of the recording booth as space where their rhymes, thoughts and feelings enable "an identity shift where they began to define themselves" (Harkness, 2014, p. 91). The analysis also revealed that artists resented notions that the studio was a place where people fooled around or partied, instead insisting serious work and emotional labor occurred. In fact, individuals who were unable to present themselves authentically and engage in deep reflection on their lived experiences within the studio were often met with criticism from their fellow artists (Harkness, 2014). The physical environment itself is imperative in this process but does not require an extraordinary budget, so long as the artists can create an environment that supports their engagement in self-discovery. In sum, the hip-hop studio itself functions as a place where artists are pushed to embrace vulnerability and emote, in order to achieve authentic personal transformation. In the following sections of this chapter, I explore a research study I engaged in, as a follow-up to the pilot study, which specifically explored a process by which a group of students constructed a studio within their school as a space for social and emotional development and a shift in school culture.

A School Counseling Office Design Study

During the 2019–2020 academic year, I collaborated with a High School in the Northeast on a HHSWT group counseling intervention whereby students built a hip-hop studio in their school. This study was written up and formally published in *The Professional Counseling* journal (Levy & Adjapong, 2020); however, the qualitative data-set (student focus group transcriptions) are re-analyzed here. The purpose of the Levy and Adjapong's (2020) study was to explore the variable of the counseling environment, asking the singular research question: *what do students report experiencing while co-creating the school studio?* This study occurred in response to the need for a process by which a school could support multicultural office design that was student centered and to develop knowledge regarding how counseling spaces for HHSWT should be constructed. To help make sense of the larger impact of studio design on students and school, in this chapter I will re-analyze the study data asking two new research questions: 1) Can hip-hop studios support student's development? and 2) Can hip-hop studios support the school community?

Studio Design Process

Over a three-month period, the hip-hop studio construction process occurred as a classroom-based school counseling intervention, within an elective hip-hop lyric writing course taught by a teacher at an urban high school in the Northeast. The class met two times per week for one hour, and 10 sessions were allocated for studio construction. As the PI for this study, I met with the elective course instructor prior to the start of the course to develop the curriculum for the studio construction process. Across a 10-week period, I stayed on as curricular support but did not facilitate the intervention. As explained in an early chapter of this text, school counselors are required to work indirectly with teachers to support their deployment of interventions that support students' social and emotional development (ASCA, 2019). In this study, I modeled this collaboration and consultation with a teacher in their use of a classroom-based school counseling intervention – i.e., the construction of a school studio as an emotional support space.

Given research detailing the cultural significance of the hip-hop studio (Harkness, 2014), calls for client-centered office design (Pearson & Wilson, 2012) and multicultural office construction (Benton & Overtree, 2012), the studio construction process was designed to be entirely student centered. The teacher's responsibility in facilitating the co-construction process was to help the group identify a goal (what the studio would look like), the roles they would play in co-construction and ultimately to keep them on task. This structure is humanistic and process-oriented in nature, providing some semblance of structure (i.e., the group would create the studio) but trusting in youth to draw from their cultural knowledge (a core construct of HHSWT) to figure out how construction would occur. Prior to the first session, the teacher and I accompanied 15 elective course students to a room where the studio would be built. Together, we prompted students to brainstorm what equipment we would need so that the teacher and I could create a GoFundMe campaign to generate necessary funding. In all, we generated $900 in donated funding to purchase the equipment that students had selected (foam pads, LED lights, a microphone, an audio interface, a beat machine, headphones, speakers and painting supplies).

Once the equipment arrived, the sessions began with a particular group structure that allowed for flexibility and trusted youth to guide the process. For example, every group opened up with a conversation about the plans for that day toward an agreement of the roles that students would play to collectively execute their design vision. To ensure that the group stayed on task, the facilitator convened the group half-way through the session to evaluate progress toward the goal for the day and pinpoint what would need to occur to wrap up the session. Each session would close with a checkout in which the group reflected on how they felt having completed the work, and what changes or additions they wanted to make during the following session. Exploratory activities were also used to allow students to reflect on environments that make them comfortable, spark conversation and work toward studio completion. As a signature assignment, the teacher pulled from the HHSWT framework and offered students the chance to create a "Where I'm From" song to support students in exploring who they are and what makes them comfortable, to generate affect content that informed their studio design decisions. Once the studio was developed, students requested assistance in learning how to use studio equipment for recording purposes. Advocating for students' requests, the teacher requested I (as a stand-in for the school counselor) visit and work with students to support their preparation toward recording their lyrics and teach students how to record their peers.

Relevant Methods

This current study will engage in a content analysis of an existing data-set to explore the potential of the hip-hop studio to support student's social and emotional development and a shift in school culture. There were 15 high school students of Black (N = 8) and Latinx (N = 7) background, ranging between 14 and 18 years of age, who participated in the original study. Data collection consisted of focus groups, after the student construction was complete, with the aim of exploring participant experiences during the studio creation. A content analysis is used here to make inferences about qualitative data relative to their specific context (in this case student development and school culture; Elo & Kyngäs, 2008). Elo and Kyngäs stated that the purpose of engaging in a content analysis was to provide new knowledge and insights. Following their work, the process in this chapter involved analyzing text into smaller categories for relevant themes through an iterative process using an inductive approach. An inductive approach "includes open coding, creating categories and abstraction" (p. 109).

Results

The findings of this study are organized by themes which emerged when analyzing the focus group transcriptions in accordance with the two research questions. Analysis resulted in a total of six themes including identifying areas of growth, maintaining authenticity, and feeling confident, advocacy and leadership, cohesion, and continuous self-work. These themes are explored below to answer the two research questions.

Research Question #1: Can Hip-Hop Studios Support Student's Development?

Data analysis yielded three themes that serve to answer the first research question: Can hip-hop studios support student's development? Emergent themes suggested studios can support students in *identifying areas of growth, maintaining authenticity and feeling confident.* Each of these themes is explored below with accompanying exemplar quotes from students as illustrations. Pseudonyms are used to mask the identities of students.

Identifying Areas of Growth

Student quotes that fall under the theme, *Identifying Areas of Growth,* speak of the power of the hip-hop studio to inspire individuals to pinpoint areas of improvement as the start of personal transformation. For example, when discussing her experience during the studio creation process, Chelsea states, "For me, I don't like public speaking. I get nervous and everything. So when I rap, because I technically have to rap in rap class, I have to stand up in front of people knowing that". In this comment, Chelsea indicates that she is uncomfortable when public speaking, but knows that by engaging in the studio during her elective course (rap class) she will confront this fear. An additional quote that illuminates this theme was from Jordan who commented:

> "I overthink a lot. I might end up thinking that they're gonna talk about me or something like that. But I feel like by the end of the day, they're not even gonna want to criticize me but they're gonna wanna be happy that I actually stood up there and rapped in front of them."

In this quote, Jordan touches on her insecurities about the thoughts of others; however, she feels that instead of receiving judgment when sharing within the studio, she believes her peers will support and validate her when she raps. This signifies that the studio space would enable Jordan to work through self-conscious feelings regarding the judgments of others. Finally, Steven shared "I just want to learn ... to speak louder. Because I'm so shy and I just want to come out of my shell", indicating that the studio space would support him in working on opening up to others and stepping outside of his comfort zone. Each of these student quotes demonstrates that students can use the studio space to identify and confront areas of personal growth. It should also be noted that the studio construction process did not entail much rapping (other than the singular "where I'm from" song); however, the construction of the studio implies that it would be a space to eventually share in. Therefore, the studio environment itself allowed students to imagine how they would grow once participating inside of it.

Maintaining Authenticity

Student quotes that fall under the second theme, *Maintaining Authenticity*, highlight how students were able to design an environment that authentically represented a hip-hop studio, and to see themselves presented authentically within that design. When reflecting on the studio design, Melissa said:

> "We chose the black for the curtains because it just looks nice and we didn't want to see all that extra storage in the back, because if we see all that extra storage it's like, it's not gonna be a studio, it's just a closet. So, we had to block that up. And then the lights, because it looked nice like a real studio, you know?"

In this comment Melissa suggests that design choices were made which maintained an authentic studio feel and involved transforming a storage closet. The specific colors were chosen to mask parts of the room that would discount the authenticity of the studio environment, and lights were placed within the room to mimic a professional studio. Beyond decor choices to create a studio environment, John offered thoughts on how students were able to portray aspects of themselves in the studio design. Specifically, he mentioned that:

> "In the studio, you could tell that there's a little piece of yourself in each sign. Like it's in a story and stuff. Like ... I don't know. Like, you could tell the story ... The foam and people working together and stuff, and like the wall. Painting it and just have their own creation and their own mind"

Through the student-led creation of the hip-hop studio, youth were able to embed pieces of themselves inside of the room which offered them a chance to tell their story. John went on to state that students could creatively distill their thoughts and feelings in a painting and the placement of foam. Ultimately, quotes from students within this theme support the conclusion that student construction of hip-hop studios enables both culturally authentic design choices and the presentation of genuine thoughts and feelings from students through design.

Feeling Confident

The third theme, *Feeling Confident,* contained statements from students indicating how prideful they felt in the studio space. For example, Devante spoke about a sense of accomplishment he felt looking back on the work the group had done, stating:

> "I love seeing how far we came from the beginning to now like, how we built this and I'm looking forward to like ... On the first day was messy and stuff and then now it's like 50% almost done. I felt like we accomplished like, we've done this."

Within the studio space, as a result of the group work, students' self-esteem can be bolstered. Alexandra explained how her confidence increased during the studio construction process, sharing, "I don't like having all the eyes on me, so I'll get a little nervous. But down here, I'm comfortable. We not that deep, we don't have a lot of people so I'm already confident with everybody here." In this quote, Alexandra shares that she used to be nervous, but feels comfortable in the studio space, partly crediting this to the smallness of the group. Lastly, Tasha stated that "I don't think there's an assignment easier than writing about yourself. You can just talk about yourself, anything. So that was a good way ... that put my confidence up a little bit." In this quote, she is discussing the process of writing a song about where she is from, which helped her feel confident in participating in the studio environment. Overall, through engaging within the studio in different capacities (building, rapping or just being in a group) students felt an increase in confidence.

Research Question #2: Can Hip-Hop Studios Support the School Community?

Data analysis yielded three themes that serve to answer the second research question: Can hip-hop studios support the school community? Emergent themes suggested that studios could support the school community with *advocacy and leadership, cohesion and continuous self-work*. Each of these themes is explored below with accompanying exemplar quotes from students to illustrate the theme.

Advocacy and Leadership

The advocacy and leadership theme pertain to student statements suggestive of leadership qualities emerging during the studio construction process. When discussing their involvement with designing the studio, Gabriel mentioned, "We decided to create a survey and send it to people from school and see what they actually like with the results. Like, we asked people, 'What would you like on the wall?'" In order to ensure that the voices of the school community were reflected within the studio space, students advocated for inclusivity by surveying the rest of the student body to gather results that would guide future design decisions. Beyond advocating for inclusive design choices, Chelsea discussed how she could engage other students in the studio to reap similar benefits. Specifically, Chelsea noted, "I feel like if freshman use this, it would help make them less shy, help them get used to coming into a new school, meeting the people, and stuff like that." After experiencing growth within the studio, students wanted to act as leaders to expose their peers to the studio's developmental benefits.

Building on these thoughts, Rachel suggested, "I feel like with this class it helped bring leaders out of us. And I don't feel like there's, person, one leader out of the group. I feel like each moment there's a different leader". In this quote Rachel describes how each student in the group was able to function as a leader during the studio construction process, illustrating student's development of leadership skills. In sum, working on studio construction supported students in exercising leadership skills and in considering how to advocate for others within the school.

Cohesion

Quotes from students further evidence the use of the school studio to promote cohesion within the larger school community. When discussing his relationship with his peers, Jay talked about how the school studio could be used to build interpersonal relationships across grade levels. In particular Jay commented that:

> "Especially this class, it helped me talk to people more and upper grades and stuff like that. Since they're also in some other classes you have with them, it helped getting to know them more better and stuff like that."

In this statement, Jay suggests that he was happy to develop relationships with students who were older than him. Additionally, Jay mentioned that while he did have other classes with these same students, working in the studio space is where rapport development occurred.

Jordan also spoke to the ability of the studio space to promote cohesiveness within the school community when she said, "You get to be surrounded by rappers and a community that knows what you're doing and you get to be upheld by everybody else and you get to share this space with everyone". Within the studio environment, it is believed that students could be surrounded by a community of like-minded peers. Student comments posited that access to this space would allow them to feel upheld and able to share with others, indicative of cohesion. Lastly, Carlos shared, "I feel like, since there's a dance team, they could actually use our rap or song and incorporate it with our dance team". Therefore, beyond using the studio space to build relationships within the school and promote a larger sense of community, the studio could be used to accentuate other school programming, such as the dance team.

Continuous Self-Work

The final theme that emerged was that the studio could offer a space within the school building where students could participate in continuous self-work. Speaking on the studio's utility as a healing space within the school community, Tasha suggested:

> "You have so many other stressing classes, you just stressing the whole day. If we could make this studio into an afterschool thing, you can just come here and just chill. Like, not worry about all the other work just for a bit. The other work, it be stressing people."

In this sense, students note the capacity of the hip-hop studio as an environment that can allow students to work through feelings of stress, almost as a means to rejuvenate before going back to class. There is also mention of creating an afterschool program. Another important quote from Devante was:

> "Before this class, let's say I'll just be in my house, just writing to a beat, or something. And then, if I'm not going to a studio, then Imma just have that, have the song written. But here, if they make this a school thing we could write out songs here and film it."

In this statement, Devante emphasizes that he had already been engaging in his own lyric writing but never had the opportunity to either share it with others, or further create through recording or filming a video. Therefore, the studio environment offered Jay the opportunity to build on the work he did outside of school, within the school building. Overall, the school studio can offer the school community a culturally aligned outlet to engage in authentic self-work and to destress.

Limitations

A few limitations to this current study exist. The size of the sample was quite small (N = 15), which resulted in only a qualitative analysis of findings. A mixed methods approach with a larger sample of students could be useful in further validating these findings. While this chapter explored the impact of a physical environment on students, it is difficult to control for this individual variable, especially when using only qualitative data. Additionally, no control group was used.

Discussing Studio Environments in HHSWT

Content analysis of focus groups on the construction process revealed a total of six themes. When questioning the impact that a school studio can have on students' development, students reported identifying areas of growth, maintaining authenticity, and feeling confident. When inquiring about the impact that school studios can have on school culture, emergent themes suggest studios promote student advocacy and leadership, cohesion, and continuous self-work.

Students highlighted the ability to identify and confront areas of personal growth, such as feelings of shyness and insecurities surrounding judgment and public speaking, within the studio environment. Similar to the current study, participants in the Harkness (2014) study reported that hip-hop studios functioned as environments for personal transformation. Further, the recording booth was found to be a physical place for individuals where rapping would lead to "an identity shift where they began to define themselves" (Harkness, 2014, p. 91). In the current study, students reported that the act of rapping in the studio could begin a personal transformation through identifying an area of growth and developing confidence in a new behavior. It is notable that many of the behavioral concerns many students faced outside of the studio (shyness, public speaking, and overthinking), appeared to dissipate within the studio itself. This finding is in alignment with past literature arguing that hip-hop cultural spaces offer participants a culturally and socially appropriate venue to address vulnerabilities they fear might otherwise be judged (Levy & Keum, 2014), and that repetition of behavior can incrementally increase self-efficacy (Bandura, 1997).

Within counseling spaces or classrooms, notions of flexibility and autonomy are of the utmost importance in supporting student development (Cook & Malloy, 2014; Huffcut, 2010; Rands & Gansemer-Topf, 2017). Within the school studio, students reported making design choices which represented a real hip-hop studio and allowed them to embed authentic parts of themselves into the decor. The authenticity of a hip-hop studio is not achieved by purchasing top-tier equipment, but is more reliant on the aesthetics of the environment which enable individuals to engage in the emotional labor necessary to create (Harkness, 2014). In current study, students created a counseling environment that felt like a real studio, and reported being able to both identify personal areas of growth and engage in the emotional labor necessary to increase self-confidence. These findings suggest that an authentic studio environment was created (Harkness, 2014), as a result of activating youth as leaders in the design process (Pearson & Wilson, 2012). Here, studio construction offers a student-centered multicultural office construction process that is missing in the literature (Benton & Overtree, 2012), and transcends the surface level and inadequate attempts to maintain cultural competence in design through the placement of multicultural art or flags on walls (Ladson-Billings, 2020; Ponterotto & Austin, 2005). In this sense, true multicultural school counseling office design requires counselors to relinquish control over the process, and position youth as leaders and bearers of the cultural knowledge necessary to design the environment. If this happens, then not only will the environment feel authentic for youth, but it will be conducive for group work which enables youth to engage in personal transformation and social and emotional development. The physical environment itself further enabled youth to infuse aspects of their authentic selves into design choices, the anthesis of colonial school practices that erase youth's internalized cultural knowledge (Emdin, 2016).

Beyond personal development, the construction of a school studio can lead to larger school culture shifts. Of note, through building the studio students reported exercising leadership skills and advocated for supporting others within the school community in using the studio space for their own development. Researchers have called for school building leaders to empower youth to act as leaders who solve problems in the school community (Siegel, 2013). There is evidence suggesting hip-hop has historically allowed avenues for participants to become community change and development leaders through advocacy work that uplift peers who share in their oppression (Forman, 2013; Levy et al., 2018). The power of hip-hop as an advocacy tool was supported by this study. Students who participated in the studio construction project reported that the environment was helpful in allowing them to destress, embrace personal concerns, develop rapport with their peers, and feel a sense of authenticity, which created an urge to invite the school community to the studio for a similar personal transformation.

Students also reported a sense of cohesion within the studio space, Therefore, beyond using the studio space to build relationships within the school and promote a larger sense of community, the school studio could be used to accentuate other school programming (i.e., a dance team or afterschool program). The school counselor's role in shifting school culture is to transcend individual student development in a way that requires them to promote student voice, and to address larger structural changes within the school community to promote equity (Hines et al., 2020; Holcomb-McCoy, 2007). The adoption of an approach to office design that is entirely student centered, and rooted in hip-hop culture, enabled the physical creation of a new environment within the students deemed culturally authentic. This structural change to the school building allowed to build relationships within the school and promote a larger sense of community, which could then lead to further systemic change through collaborations with the school clubs, teams and programs. Lastly, the hip-hop studio was viewed by students within the school as a place for continuous self-work. School counselors need to function as leaders within the school building, developing school wide interventions that support the social and emotional development of all students (Bowers et al., 2018). The establishment of the studio offered the school a physical location for students to destress. Students reported bringing rhymes with them to school, which would have otherwise stayed in their bedroom, to share with classmates. The act of bringing parts of self to school, which one otherwise would not, exemplifies the power of the studio as a physical space that invites authentic expression and supports schools in circumventing oppressive practices that might squelch this very type of expression.

Implications

Although not explored in the original pilot study (Levy, 2019), this follow-up study looked specifically at counseling office design as an important variable in the healing process. These findings have powerful implications for the field of school counseling. Of note, social and emotional group work wherein students engaging in writing, recording and performing emotionally themed hip-hop songs can be accentuated through the co-construction of a physical counseling environment. School counselors and teachers can collaborate with youth in co-construction, opening up the studio environment to support both classroom, small group, and individual counseling interventions. The current study helped to concretize a youth-driven process that educators can follow in their attempts to construct school studios for social and emotional development support.

There are also implications for the use of school studios to spur larger changes in school culture. Results indicated that students had just scratched the surface of what the studio could be used for within the school, implying that the more the studio is developed and used on a daily basis, the more collaborative opportunities will emerge that aid the development of school culture. What is arguably most important here is that this entire process was guided by youth, which implies a trust in youth to identify parts of the school system that need to be altered to create inclusive environments. School counselors are often eager to engage in systemic changes within the school building to support the outcomes of all students, but seldom consider relinquishing their control to put students in a position of power to guide that work. This study implies that when given control, students can find answers, to issues we are yet to adequately solve. It is inherently humanistic and supportive of Black and Brown voice.

Conclusion

In this chapter, I present the importance of hip-hop studio construction in aiding the development of students and school culture. This chapter introduces studio construction as a salient element in HHSWT. Chapter 5 will explore another missing variable from the pilot study, which is the use of hip-hop mixtape making to guide the counseling process. This will include an overview of theoretical constructions of mixtape making in HHSWT followed by qualitative and quantitative data speaking to the impact of mixtape making on young people.

References

American School Counselor Association [ASCA]. (2019). *The ASCA national model: A framework for school counseling programs* (4th ed.). American School Counselor Association.

Bandura, A. (1997). The anatomy of stages of change. *American Journal of Health Promotion, 12*(1), 8–10. DOI: 10.4278/0890-1171-12.1.8

Barber, J. (2006). Eckerd college: Peter H. Armacost library. In D. Oblinger (Ed.), *Learning spaces.* Retrieved from www.educause.edu/learningspaces

Benton, J. M., & Overtree, C. E. (2012). Multicultural office design: A case example. *Professional Psychology: Research and Practice, 43*(3), 265. doi:10.1037/a0027443

Bowers, H., Lemberger-Truelove, M. E., & Brigman, G. (2018). A social-emotional leadership framework for school counselors. *Professional School Counseling, 21*(1b).

Brewe, E., Kramer, L., & Sawtelle, V. (2012). Investigating student communities with network analysis of interactions in a physics learning center. *Physical Review Special Topics-Physics Education Research, 8*(1). doi:10.1103/PhysRevSTPER.8.010101

Ceylan, C., Dul, J., & Aytac, S. (2008). Can the office environment stimulate a manager's creativity? *Human Factors and Ergonomics in Manufacturing & Service Industries, 18*(6), 589–602. https://doi.org/10.1002/hfm.20128

Cook, K., & Malloy, L. (2014). School counseling office design: Creating safe space. *Journal of Creativity in Mental Health, 9*(3), 436–443. doi:10.1080/15401383.2014.890557

Cook, A. L., Levy, I., & Whitehouse, A. (2020). Exploring youth participatory action research in urban schools: Advancing social justice and equity-based counseling practices. *Journal for Social Action in Counseling & Psychology, 12*(1), 27–43.

Devlin, A. S., Borenstein, B., Finch, C., Hassan, M., Iannotti, E., & Koufopoulos, J. (2013). Multicultural art in the therapy office: Community and student perceptions of the therapist. *Professional Psychology: Research and Practice, 44*(3), 168. doi:10.1037/a0031925

Duckworth, C., Albano, T., Munroe, D., & Garver, M. (2019). "Students can change a school": Understanding the role of youth leadership in building a school culture of peace. *Conflict Resolution Quarterly, 36*(3), 235–249.

Elo, S., & Kyngäs, H. (2008). The qualitative content analysis process. *Journal of advanced nursing, 62*(1), 107–115. doi: 10.1111/j.1365-2648.2007.04569

Emdin, C. (2016). *For White folks who teach in the hood... and the rest of y'all too: Reality pedagogy and urban education.* Beacon Press.

Emdin, C. (2010). Affiliation and alienation: Hip-hop, rap, and urban science education. *Journal of Curriculum Studies, 42*(1), 1–25. doi:10.1080/00220270903161118

Forman, M. (2013). 'Hood Work: Hip-Hop, Youth Advocacy, and Model Citizenry. *Communication, Culture & Critique, 6*(2), 244–257. https://doi.org/10.1111/cccr.12012

Goelitz, A., & Stewart-Kahn, A. S. (2008). Therapeutic use of space: One agency's transformation project. *Journal of Creativity in Mental Health, 2*(4), 31–44.

Hall, G. E., & Hord, S. M. (2015). *Implementing change: Patterns, principles, and potholes.* Pearson Education.

Hannigan, S., Grima-Farrell, C., & Wardman, N. (2019). Drawing on creative arts therapy approaches to enhance inclusive school cultures and student wellbeing. *Issues in Educational Research, 29*(3), 756–773.

Hansen, J. T., Speciale, M., & Lemberger, M. E. (2014). Humanism: The foundation and future of professional counseling. *The Journal of Humanistic Counseling, 53*(3), 170–190. doi:10.1002/j.2161-1939.2014.00055.x

Harkness, G. (2014). Get on the mic: Recording studios as symbolic spaces in rap music. *Journal of Popular Music Studies, 26*(1), 82–100. doi:10.1111/jpms.12061

Hines, E. M., Moore III, J. L., Mayes, R. D., Harris, P. C., Vega, D., Robinson, D. V., ... & Jackson, C. E. (2020). Making student achievement a priority: The role of school counselors in turnaround schools. *Urban Education, 55*(2), 216–237. doi:10.1177/0042085916685761

Holcomb-McCoy, C. C. (2007). *School counseling to close the achievement gap: A Social justice framework for success.* Thousand Oaks, CA: Corwin.

Huffcut, J. C. (2010). Can design promote healing? *Behavioral Healthcare, 30*(9), 33–35. Retrieved from http://www.behavioral.net/article/can-design-promote-healing/

Hunley, S. & Schaler, M. (2006). Assessing learning spaces. In D. Oblinger (Ed.), *Learning spaces.* Retrieved from www.educause.edu/learningspaces

Imms, W., & Byers, T. (2017). Impact of classroom design on teacher pedagogy and student engagement and performance in mathematics. *Learning Environments Research, 20*(1), 139–152. doi:10.1007/s10984-016-9210-0

Ladson-Billings, G. (2020). *Building culturally relevant schools.* Lecture.

Lewis, J., Asberry, J., DeJarnett, G., & King, G. (2016). The best practices for shaping school culture for instructional leaders. *Alabama Journal of Educational Leadership, 3,* 57–63.

Levy, I. (2019). Hip-hop and spoken word therapy in urban school counseling. *Professional School Counseling, 22*(1b).

Levy, I. (2020). "Real Recognize Real: Hip-Hop Spoken Word Therapy and Humanistic Practice. *The Journal of Humanistic Counseling, 59*(1), 38–53. https://doi.org/10.1002/johc.12128

Levy, I., & Adjapong, E. S. (2020). Toward culturally competent school counseling environments: Hip-hop studio construction. *Professional Counselor, 10*(2), 266–284. Retrieved from https://files.eric.ed.gov/fulltext/EJ1259697.pdf

Levy, I., Cook, A. L., & Emdin, C. (2018). Remixing the school counselor's tool kit: Hip hop spoken word therapy and YPAR. *Professional School Counseling, 22*(1), doi:10.1177/2156759X18800285

Levy, I., & Keum, B. T. (2014). Hip hop emotional exploration in men. *Journal of Poetry Therapy, 27*(4), 217–223. doi:10.1080/08893675.2014.949528

Liddicoat, S. (2010). Counselling workspace design and therapeutic practice. 10.

Liddicoat, S. (2015) *Exploring relations between body, communication and agency in therapeutic space. Living and Learning: Research for a Better Built Environment: 49th International Conference of the Architectural,* Melbourne, Australia.

Martin, P. J. (2015). Transformational thinking in today's schools. In B. Erford (Ed.), *Transforming the school counseling profession* (4 ed., pp. 45–65). Upper Saddle River, NJ: Pearson Education.

Miwa, Y., & Hanyu, K. (2006). The effects of interior design on communication and impressions of a counselor in a counseling room. *Environment and Behavior, 38*(4), 484–502. doi:10.1177/0013916505280084

Monahan, T. (2000). Built pedagogies and technological practices: Designing for participatory learning. Referenced from http://torinmonahan.com/papers/pdc2000.pdf

Monahan, T. (2002). Flexible space and built pedagogy: Emerging IT embodiments. *Inventio, 4* (1): 1–19.

Pearson, M., & Wilson, H. (2012). Soothing spaces and healing places: Is there an ideal counselling room design? *Psychotherapy in Australia, 18*(3), 46. Retrieved from http://markpearson.com.au/pdf/pearson-wilson_ideal_counselling_rooms_2012.pdf

Ponterotto, J. G., & Austin, R. (2005). Emerging approaches to training psychologists to be culturally competent. In R. T. Carter (Ed.), *Handbook of racial-cultural psychology and counseling.* Wiley.

Pressly, P. K., & Heesacker, M. (2001). The physical environment and counseling: A Review of theory and research. *Journal of Counseling & Development, 79*(2), 148–160. doi:10.1002/j.1556-6676.2001.tb01954.x

Rands, M. L., & Gansemer-Topf, A. M. (2017). The room itself is active: How classroom design impacts student engagement. *Journal of Learning Spaces, 6*(1), 26.

Rogers, S. L., Edwards, S. J., & Perera, R. (2018). The impact of shared versus individual office space on therapist appraisal of their work environment. Asia-Pacific *Journal of Health Management, 13*(1), i26-i26.

Sanders, M. (2013). Classroom design and student engagement. *Proceedings of the Human Factors and Ergonomics Society Annual Meeting 2013 57*: 496. DOI: 10.1177/1541931213571107

Sanders, R., & Lehmann, J. (2018). An exploratory study of clients' experiences and preferences for counselling room space and design. *Counselling and Psychotherapy Research.* doi:10.1002/capr.12202

Siegel, D. J. (2013). *Brainstorm: The power and purpose of the teenage brain.* New York: Penguin Putnam.

Sleegers, P., Moolenaar, N., Galetzka, M., Pruyn, A., Sarroukh, B. & Zande, B. (2012). Lighting affects students' concentration positively: Findings from three Dutch studies. *Lighting Research and Technology, 45*(2), 159–175.

5 Mixtape-Making
Leveraging the Power of Youth Participatory Action Research

Mixtape-Making: Leveraging the Power of Youth Participatory Action Research

Beyond the relationships I felt able to build with students while using HHWST, and the physical studio we created, students wrote hip-hop lyrics during the group process. The main quantitative finding from the HHSWT pilot study (Levy, 2019) is perhaps reflective of this, showing that students learned to use lyric writing as a coping mechanism. That is, through writing, recording and performing emotionally themed hip-hop music, students worked through emotional stressors. Within the group work process however, separate from those reported outcomes, were a series of steps students took to create a cohesive collection of songs that they recorded, marketed and shared with the school and personal communities. As a facilitator, students schooled me on the intricacies of both developing a body of work (transcending the mere creation of a few songs) and the necessary tasks one must engage into property market the work. This, they called a mixtape.

A *mixtape* is a collection of songs that form a full body of work and are often used by artists as a means to uplift their own voices and share untold stories (Ball, 2011) – for example, during the HHSWT group student conversations centered on the theme of police brutality, exploring a variety of current and past cases of the unjust killings of Black people by police officers. These conversations, spurred by the inundation of media images students endured, organically lead to the creation of individual songs about police brutality. The initial conversation, specifically about the death of Mike Brown in Ferguson, MI, led students to develop a list of topics they wanted to address. A handful of these topics were individual cases that emerged before or during group conversations (i.e., the deaths of Travon Martin, Sandra Bland and Walter Scott), but also included students writing about their own experiences with police. A single song on the project discussed the impact of racial bias on their daily life, where another asked the important question of "How do we find peace?" amidst injustice. Simply put, each individual track was different, yet connected, to the singular mixtape theme of police brutality. When the songs were all complete, the students advocated for the physical creation of CDs that they could sell to friends, family, teachers and peers. Students hosted a bake sale at the school and developed a local community donation campaign to generate funding for the physical CDs. Additionally, students requested that I (as their school counselor) set up a show at the school and search for opportunities within the community to perform. This subsequently led to a school show and fieldtrips to a couple of local colleges and universities where the students shared their music. The project-oriented nature of mixtape-making emerged naturally throughout the group work process and was both student-centered and unpredictable.

Most importantly however, this process was not explicitly explored in the initial pilot study. In the original study, pre- and post-course surveys assessed student's emotional self-awareness, coping skills and stress, but did not attempt to capture how the components of mixtape-making impacted student outcome data. Therefore, in Chapter 5 I aim to explore the intricacies of hip-hop mixtape-making as a group work process. I will explore mixtape-making theoretically, practically and empirically, and then close with engaging in the analysis of student lyrics from two separate mixtapes.

Theory on Group Counseling Curriculum

The functionality of counseling groups has received much focus within the literature. One functionality domain is that of group type, where scholars discuss the different uses of content and process groups (Gladding, 2019; Sink et al., 2011; Yalom & Leszcz, 2005). Simply put, content groups are structured with defined activities that guide group counseling sessions. In contrast, process groups rely more on the "here and now" and believe in allowing the group to work through questions in real-time and determine a group goal (Gladding, 2019). Developmental considerations are important when determining the ideal group type in that content groups are recommended for younger children and process groups are said to be more useful at a high school level where students have the cognitive capacity to sit-in and sort through emotional concerns (Sink et al., 2011). Group types, however, exist on a spectrum and often contain structured activities (content) as well as moments of here-and-now reflection (process), with variations that lean toward either end (Gladding, 2019).

Related to group type is the idea of group facilitation style, or the facilitators' conceptualization of their role within the group. There is a lack of certainty regarding which leadership style is most facilitative of positive outcomes for youth (Chen, & Rybak, 2017; Gladding, 2019; Milsom, 2018). An authoritarian group leader utilizes a structured approach in which they lead the group counseling process, minute-by-minute.

They might use a lesson plan and keep to a strict structure (Hogg & Adelman, 2013). Conversely, laissez-faire group facilitators see themselves as immersed within the group process hoping to help the group decide on their own group goals, and then to only assist them in focusing on that goal (Gladding, 2019). Pulling from both the authoritarian and laissez-faire group facilitation styles, the democratic leadership approach to group counseling positions the facilitator as an equal partner in the group counseling process who assembles a loose structure (content activities) but is ready and willing to abandon structure when the group wants to go a different direction (process; Milsom, 2018).

Generally, there are valid concerns from researchers and practitioners regarding lack of student-centered group counseling in schools that minimize youth engagement in session (Smith et al., 2014). Hip-hop scholarship has long critiqued defined curriculum, pedagogical or counseling, in that cookie-cutter lesson plans may similarly stifle youth voice and disallow prolonged cultural relevance (Petchauer, 2009; Rose, 2018). In short, there is a need for hip-hop-based approaches in education that transcend asking students to watch music videos or write raps, and instead foster an understanding of how hip-hop aesthetics and sensibilities, germane to hip-hop culture broadly, benefit students' development (Rose, 2018). Within hip-hop and counseling group work, there is minimal literature exploring what types of groups or facilitation styles are preferable in different contexts (Levy & Travis, 2020), and how allowing youth to guide sessions might enable their use of hip-hop culture to transform group process (Levy et al., 2018).

YPAR in Group Work

When determining what a hip-hop-based group process looks like, it is reasonable to consider the use of Youth Participatory Action Research (YPAR), which is presented as an alternative group counseling approach that activates youth as partners or co-researchers (Smith et al., 2010). In YPAR, youth lead the process of research and group work by pinpointing specific issues they would like to address (Hipolito-Delgado & Lee, 2007), a direct shift away from students being the passive recipients of counseling (Smith et al., 2014). Considering facilitation, YPAR intentionally blurs these roles in order for youth to function as leaders and bolster their self-efficacy for taking action in social change (Hipolito-Delgado & Lee, 2007). During YPAR group sessions youth collaborate as active leaders with their school counselor to identify a research topic, choose a focus for a project, develop research methods, collect data and develop a research dissemination plan (Cook & Krueger-Henney; 2017; Singh et al., 2012; Smith et al., 2010).

The dissemination of research projects through YPAR offers schools and students a medium for community engagement (Smith et al., 2010).

Through YPAR work, youth have collaborated with school administration (Kohfeldt et al., 2011; Smith et al., 2010), the community (Berg et al., 2009; Jennings et al., 2006; Wilson et al., 2008) and have used online platforms (Ozer & Wright, 2012) for the dissemination of their projects. Creative approaches to YPAR dissemination include using technology to share findings (Cammarota & Fine, 2008; Smith et al., 2010), photovoice to share student narratives as research (Del Vecchio et al., 2017), hosting community events, writing blog posts, creating artwork or creating and performing music (Berg et al., 2009; Jennings et al., 2006; Levy et al., 2018; Ozer & Wright, 2012; Wilson et al., 2008). Ultimately, integrating YPAR into a group counseling process supports youth in actively exploring and developing solutions for issues of personal relevance to them (Cook & Krueger-Henney, 2017; Singh et al., 2012).

Hip-hop Mixtapes

In HHSWT, the *hip-hop mixtape-making* is a distinct creation of a hip-hop cultural product that has value within YPAR and can guide the group counseling process. Scholars describe that mixtapes are commonly created by new emcees over popular hip-hop beats to boast their lyrical talent and promote their individual voice (Ball, 2011; Pulley, 2010). Mixtapes are credited as playing a pivotal role in the growth of hip-hop culture, particularly in amplifying minimized voices which spoke back against systemic inequities (Ball, 2009, 2011). Ball (2011) explains that the "mixtape's origins are grassroots and countercultural" (p. 285) and have offered culturally salient pathways for Black and Brown communities to express, process and push back against larger systems of colonialism and imperialism. Based on the need to offer culturally sensitive group counseling process that is youth centered, the hip-hop mixtape process should be considered for group work. Considering the establishment and dissemination of hip-hop mixtapes at the community level, there appears to be an organic overlap with YPAR. In the remainder of this chapter I will explore a theoretical framework for the school counselor's use of mixtapes in YPAR work, followed by practical and empirical insights, and an analysis of student lyrics.

The Critical Cycle of Mixtape Creation

Given the need for group work that is culturally responsive, youth centered and enables hip-hop hop culture to manifest organically, I argue it becomes essential to engage youth in the creation of mixtapes about emotional themes of importance to them. Therefore, I believe we must infuse mixtape-making with YPAR to establish both a counseling model and practice wherein youth conduct action research and dissemination around issues they deem relevant. This process is called the Critical Cycle of Mixtape Creation (CCMC). Drawing from the YPAR cycle of investigative inquiry (Cook & Krueger-Henney, 2017), school counselors facilitate a series of emotional discussions that aid youth in research, discussing, writing and recording a series of songs following a series of steps which guide the counseling process, including *Identify Action Mixtape Area of Interest, Research Mixtape Content, Discuss and Digest Findings, Develop a Tracklist, Plan the Recording and Release of Mixtape* and *Evaluate Mixtape Process and Response to Release.* These steps are explained in detail in the following sections.

Identify Action Mixtape Area of Interest

In the CCMC, the specific content of the emotionally themed mixtape functions as the youth-selected research topic that guides the counseling process. Drawing from YPAR, mixtape themes can include a variety of topics including psychological health and well-being, social/environmental factors, academic issues or anything of interest to students. Important in the mixtape-making process is that a single theme selected by students can be divided into a medley of songs that explore that theme from different vantage points. For example, the mixtape theme of stress can include songs on school, home life, friends, future goals and more. It is important that mixtape themes are complex enough to research and develop related themes for individual songs. Levy and Travis (2020) created an activity where youth designed and shared out an artist profile containing information like their artist name, favorite food and topics they like to write about. Activities like the artist profile offer school counselors the opportunity to actively listen and highlight possible broad topics for the mixtape, considering what concepts they want to address as an artist, and subthemes for individual songs on the project.

Research Mixtape Content

After students select their mixtape area of interest, they transition into collecting data, or conducting research, on their topic. A variety of activities can be created which support this process, not limited to tasking students with analyzing existing hip-hop songs and/or music videos, podcasts, new reports, blog posts or articles, or public interviews (with or without artists). Students might choose to interview family members about a topic to generate content for a specific song. Within the context of a school, students might even decide to develop a survey which helps them collect data on a given issue from either their peers, teachers or other school staff. Research is also not limited to collecting external data. The use of self-reflection or self-analysis as an internal research process is also crucial. To this end, school counselors should encourage students to reflect on personal experiences they have had with the topic of interest (i.e., stress). The collection of data in the CCMC process supports the eventual construction of songs on the mixtape.

Discuss and Digest Findings

Once students have completed their research, the counselor brings the group together to share and digest the findings. This stage of the process is again quite flexible in facilitation in that students can share PowerPoint presentations on their findings, produce a written document or present a video/picture montage which details what they have discovered. Students should be offered the opportunity to decide how they share their findings with the group. Discussing and digesting the research findings offers the group space to observe their mixtape theme from multiple angles and concretize their approach to selecting subtopics and constructing lyrics on their mixtape. In prior group work practice, I have tasked students with creating brief proposals (an explanation of the concept, a potential beat, research support and a data collection strategy) for a song topic and sharing it with the group for their approval.

Develop a Tracklist

The analysis of findings leads organically to the development of a tracklist for the mixtape. In this stage students not only determine the different subthemes they will address on individual mixtape tracks but also negotiate their roles. Students may decide they want to work on songs individually or collaborate with each other. The school counselor supports students in co-defining roles, allowing them to break into subgroups to work on a variety of songs or to work independently. Students may also decide they do not want to write lyrics but have talent in producing a beat, designing the artwork for the mixtape or creating flyers and social media content to promote the project. Students should have the autonomy to select roles where they feel comfortable. In collaborative work, students can be encouraged to engage in role-play exercises where they co-construct a song about a shared emotional experience. For example, if students were writing about navigating tension with friends or family members, the counselor can ask two students to write a verse where they role-play engaging in a difficult conversation together. Similarly, drawing from a gestalt tactic of "the empty chair" school counselors can task students with sitting in front of an empty chair or a mirror and writing self-reflective songs where they imagine confronting an intra- or interpersonal conflict.

Plan the Recording and Release of Mixtape

After the various tracks have been identified, group members begin to *plan the recording and release of the mixtape*. During this stage, the group has a formal "meeting" where they decide on the title of the mixtape, the tracks that need to be recorded (potentially listing "due dates" for each track) and the album artwork. The group will also discuss a promotional plan, which includes the possible release of "singles" (songs released prior to the album to generate excitement for the project), a plan for releasing the album (posting music online versus creating physical copies) and whether or not they would like to schedule a mixtape release party (where artists perform their album for the first time). The group will also consider how the dissemination of their mixtape might have positively impacted their selected issue. If students were writing about stress, they may have a listening party for the school where they both perform their mixtape for the student body and talk about the meaning behind the tracks, in attempt to help their student body experience stress reduction. Once these details are ironed out, the group then breaks into smaller subgroups and works on individual tracks. While the group may come back together to share what they have written and receive feedback, the purpose is to execute the writing, recording and release of the mixtape.

Evaluate Mixtape Process and Response to Release

During the final step of CMCC, the group has completed their plan for the recording and release of their mixtape and will then *evaluate the mixtape process and response to the mixtape release*. The group might discuss the "highs" and "lows" of the CMCC process to inform adjustments for their next mixtape. If the group performed their mixtape, they may want to watch the film of their performance to assess their showcase and discuss reactions from the audience. The school counselor might pose questions like, "Did our lyrics about important issues resonate with the audience in the way we hoped?", or "How could we have been more effective in sharing our music with our audience?" The group can also refer back to their dissemination plan and assess whether or not their research, release and/or performance of their mixtape had the change they hoped for. If students hoped their project would help their peers feel less stressed, did they accomplish this goal? Students might consider sending out a follow-up survey after the listening party to assess this goal. Overall, the CMCC process allows a group to identify an issue of importance for them and proceed to research, write, record and disseminate their findings and/or solutions in a culturally relevant and youth-driven capacity.

Assessing the CCMC in Practice

During the summer of 2019, I collaborated with a colleague (Dr. Raphael Travis, professor of social work at Texas State University-San Marcos) on the implementation of the CCMC model, assessing its impact on student's well-being (i.e., stress, depression and anxiety). Together we spent five days with a small group (N=18) of youth who were attending a summer enrichment program at a university in the Southwest. Data was collected around this group intervention that was published in the *Journal of Specialists in Group Work* (Levy & Travis, 2020). The results of the CCMC study are shared here to describe the impact the CCMC model on youth development. With an interest in assessing the efficacy of different group counseling facilitation styles, we designed three separate groups (six students in each) that would take students through the CCMC process. Each day of the five total days aligned with a stage of the model: Day 1: *Identify Action Mixtape Area of Interest*, Day 2: *Research Mixtape Content*, Day 3: *Discuss and Digest Findings, Develop a Tracklist*, Day 4: *Plan the Recording and Release of Mixtape* and Day 5: *Evaluate Mixtape Process and Response to Release.*

The first group was facilitated with an authoritarian group leadership style, where the co-facilitators led the group through minute-by-minute activities, guiding them toward making a social justice-themed song (Youth wished to explore the theme of immigration in their song). Students did not have a choice on this social justice topic area, as the facilitators made that choice in order to align themselves with the authoritarian style. The second group was facilitated using a democratic leadership, still using the CMCC model, but instead youth compiled a list of potential topics and voted on them. Aligned with the democratic leadership style, the theme of the hip-hop song could have been about any issue of importance to them, allowing a collaborative approach. Youth chose to construct a song about their personal and future life goals. Lastly, the third group was facilitated using a laissez-faire style where youth were intentionally allowed full control over designing their own hip-hop project about any topic that they mutually agreed would be of interest for them to explore. The facilitators worked to step back from the CCMC process, reminding the group only of how much time they had left to meet their agreed-upon goal (which in this group was to create a song and music video about relationships). The facilitators were part of the process in that we supported youth when they asked for it, but a leadership decision was made to attempt to not guide the group in any way.

Data in the Levy & Travis (2020) study were collected using a pre- and post-group survey measuring well-being (i.e., stress, depression and anxiety). This study concluded significant decreases among the entire sample (N = 18) for both stress and depression, but not for anxiety. So, regardless of leadership style the full sample of students benefited from the CCMC process. However, an analysis of youth outcomes by leadership style, *autorotation* (n = 6) vs. *democratic* (n = 6) vs. *laissez-faire* (n = 6), indicated that only the democratic group participants experienced a statistically significant reduction in stress. In this sense, while all group leadership styles were helpful the democratic or choice-based group process was most conducive of positive outcomes, which counters notions that authoritarian (Gladding, 2019; Sink et al., 2011) or full youth-driven processes (Milsom, 2018) are most appropriate for adolescents.

A Content Analysis of Two Mixtapes

In the introduction to this chapter I shared a narrative of students creating their own mixtape. This narrative was followed by a review of group curriculum and leadership design literature and a preference for YPAR as a youth-guided group process. The CCMC, building on existing knowledge of hip-hop mixtapes as a cultural product, was shared in order to detail theoretical and empirical evidence of a hip-hop-based approached to YPAR. Data from an evaluation study supported the conclusion that by engaging in the CCMC process youth experienced reductions in feelings of stress, depression and anxiety. Interestingly, while youth explored a medley of different to emotional concerns during group work (feelings surrounding the social justice issue of immigration, personal and future goals, and relationships), the full sample still experienced improvements in well-being. The apparent flexibility of the mixtape-making process (both with regard to the facilitation style and the selection of mixtape content) is an important takeaway in that it suggests mixtape-making might offer counselors a flexible framework for addressing a range of emotions that youth bring with them into session. To further assess this mailability the goal of this follow-up study was to deepen our understanding of the emotional content students unearth while creating mixtapes. Therefore, this section uses a content analysis to investigate two mixtapes asking a singular research question: *When engaging in mixtape-making, what content do students focus on?*

Relevant Methods

To engage in this content analysis, I accessed two mixtapes my students created during group work during the 2016–2017 school year (i.e., the pilot program), titled The Hoodies Up Mixtape (21 songs) and the Adolescence Mixtape (16 songs). As per the demographic data shared in chapter 2 regarding the pilot study, 12 students participated in groups where these mixtapes were created – half of whom identified as Black and 9 were identified as male. Both of the mixtapes were available on Soundcloud (a popular and free, online, music sharing website), along with album artwork that visually represented the tone of each project. The album artwork is available in Figure 5.1. A total of 36 songs were transcribed and transferred to a Word document for word-by-word

Hoodies Up Mixtape	**Adolescent Mixtape**

Figure 5.1 Mixtape Artwork

Note. The artwork for Hoodies Up Mixtape, centering on police brutality, pays homage to
 Trayvon Martin who was unjustly killed by George Zimmerman. The artwork for the
 Adolescence Mixtape, focusing on the development of adolescents generally, highlights the introspective and emotional work students engaged in while writing and
 recording their songs.

identifying, labeling and eventually categorizing themes. Customary in
content analysis (Elo & Kyngäs, 2008), I drew inferences about what topics students explored in mixtape-making and used open coding to create
categories that define the content students wrote about. Coding techniques were used, including audit trails, to ensure trustworthiness of
data and credibility of recurring themes (Creswell, 2013).

Results

Over the course of a singular school year (2016–2017) two separate
counseling groups (during the 1st and 2nd semesters respectively)
followed the CCMC and created mixtapes about a specific topic. The
first group as alluded to in the introduction to this chapter, titled their
project the Hoodies Up mixtape which had a board focus on police brutality. The second group of students wished to create a project around a
different theme and chose the topic of Adolescence. Both of these mixtapes were explored using the research question: *When analyzing lyrics on
two mixtapes, what do students report experiencing?* Results illuminate both
the Hoodies Up and Adolescence mixtape offered youth a venue to
explore a slew of thoughts and feelings during group work. Song titles,
themes and sample lyrics from each mixtape are explored below to portray the variety of emotions students processed.

Hoodies Up Mixtape

The Hoodies Up Mixtape sought to explore police brutality as a construct. Analysis revealed that each of the 21 songs on this project explored
a particular emotional theme that could be grouped into four larger
categories describing the general subject: *Policing, Overcoming Struggle,*

Impacting Others, Reflecting on Life Experiences. Each song title, category and theme provided in Table 5.1.

Policing. A total of five songs on this mixtape focused on Policing directly. The students opened their mixtape with a song titled "5'0 Gotta Know" that called police out on specific cases in which unarmed Black men were wrongfully murdered. For example, one student rapped, *"This is the basis justice for Mike Brown, Trayvon and Jordan Davis. Murdered by old racist in prolonged cases and trials all the while dead bodies getting piled by cops with a smile in a single file".* Other songs on the project again focused directly on police brutality, like Revolution which boasts lyrics such as *"Buffoonery seen in movements of 5'0 not knowing what they doing./Cut the music revolution is leading towards pollution and confusion an illusion./Used to ignite a fuse and recite the blues",* signifying that youth wished to expose injustice to spur change. On their song, Goodtimes, students tried considering how to remain positive and personally overcome the stress associated with said killings. Goodtimes contained lyrics like:

> "The White man repeating the past, shooting people that have color contrast,/the memory is vast almost like my last class,/but I clear my mind fast, forgot the past and try to graduate at the top of my class."

Table 5.1 Hoodies Up Mixtape Tracklist by Title, Category and Theme

Song Titles	Song Themes
Policing (category)	
5'0 Gotta Know	Frustration with Police
Peace	Combating hate and racism
Goodtimes	Overcoming social issues
Revolution	Exposing inequity
Overcoming Struggle (category)	
Nikes	Perseverance
Be Who You Be	Determination
Survival	Empowerment
Represent	Pride
One Dream	Future goals
Impacting Others (category)	
Ride or Die	Support systems
Role Model	Finding inspiration
Boutta Be Done Soon	Leveraging the mind and intellect
Sleepless	Promoting awareness of injustice
Music Saved Us	Sharing the power of music
Reflections (category)	
My Life	Reflections on salient life events
It's Whatever Tho	Navigating relationships
State of Mind	Cultivating focus
Places & Places Remix	Exploring hidden places in the mind
From Time	Reminiscing on the past

Group members also wished to create a song called Peace which sought to combat hatred stemming from racism in the world and internally, writing a chorus that stated, *"I want peace in the world, peace in every nation. /Peace is the only thing that contradicts hatred"*.

Overcoming Struggle. Through their research and development of the mixtape tracklist, students pinpointed five different song topics related to police brutality. For example, students believed that determination was necessary amidst the brevity and fragility of life and penned the song, Be Who You Be, which had lyrics like:

> "Life is too damn short can't be worried bout others/I'll keep grinding for my sista, my mother, and my brothers, no other motivation and dedication is key,/don't let these snakes get in ya head just be who you be".

Rhymes on the song Nikes described perseverance amidst obstacles, *"It's all about the grind keeping my grades up,/I was cold so then I gassed that internal flame up."* On Survival students tapped into struggle as a means for empowerment. An exemplar rhyme from this song details leveraging struggle as a form of experiential knowledge that can be used for success:

> "I'm self-made survival is what I know, /
> had nobody to help me and put me on the right road./
> So, I had to struggle and overcome adversity,/
> my thoughts are worth millions so I use them as some currency./
> My thoughts are put in books all over your university."

Songs like Represent described the physical environments youth were raised in, and a sense of pride they felt, *"Representing New York City wasn't born in but raised, where everybody killing or just tryna paid, I got away, ditched left now yah stuck like a maze, haters all ways of your back that's just part of the day"*. Lastly, One Dream was a song where students detailed how difficult emotional experiences solidified future goals:

> "Before I lost my momma, when I was still crawlin,/
> she had a dream that I was gonna be ballin like Jordan./
> Y'all trying to be patient, man I'm just trying to make it./
> I know we both on earth but your mind is in the matrix."

Impacting Others. Through a series of five songs on the project, students portrayed complex versions of themselves that aimed to transcend stereotypical perceptions they believed police held of them and their culture. For example, a song titled Music Saved Us described the power of hip-hop music that is often overshadowed, *"You see I studied others music so that I could make art, I was inspired by the masterpieces that came* *from their hearts. Hip-hop is another langue that some just can't decipher..."* On Boutta Be Done Soon, a student recited rhymes about his intellect being overlooked, *"I wake up see struggle around me/now you clown's see why it's good to act wisely around me. /People despise me cuz they know a smart mind is exactly what they really need".* The track Sleepless attempted to inform others how inequity operates, *"Not new to the system and how it works./ It's used to keep you down and keep you straight outta work..."* On songs Ride or Die students urged listeners to develop strong support systems, and therefore wrote a chorus stating, *"It's always good to have someone there by your side/recognizes you and fills you up with pride./Even if it's nighttime they could make you shine./ They can be other half they can be yah ride or die".* Similarly, the song Role Models encouraged others to find people who offer inspiration as a means to traverse life's difficulties, *"Who's your role model in this world?/ Could be a guy or could be a girl./Inspires your to chase your dreams/Spitting this rap hope yah know what I mean."*

Reflections. The final six songs on the mixtape were reflections on past life experiences that serve as a blueprint for navigating future struggles. A specific song called My Life was composed of rhymes that concretized life lessons:

> "When I was 8 years old, I figured my goal/
> To get my grandma anything that she want in this world/
> So I was never alone, she taught me right from wrong,
> she was there for me when my parents didn't care at all."

Additionally, student's distilled advice from how they navigated prior relationships on their song It's Whatever Tho – *"Friends can be the first to stab you in the back./To say it ain't true but it's really just a fact./Pulled that lame excuse from scratch".* Furthering their introspection, students produced a song (Places) and a remix (Places Remix) that contained lyrics exploring hidden thoughts and feelings within their minds, *"Different places in my mind, places that bind me together all the time./Dark, gloomy, bright and little places, a trace from the past my past is like a legend".* Students used the song From Time to reminisce on past mistakes and grievances, rapping, *"Thinking bout how I did wrong and how it changed my life,/And everyday I think about it - it just get me tight,/So I wanna change my life and do the right things,/loose strings to tight strings".* Finally, the song State of Mind described the cultivation of focus through reflection – *"I'm doing what I have to till I'm getting mine,/I got my brothers when I'm outta line, rhyming till see the sun rise that's just my state of mind".*

Adolescence Mixtape

The Adolescence Mixtape sought to explore student's development during adolescence. Analysis revealed that each of the 16 songs on this project explored a particular emotional theme, related to adolescent development. These songs could be grouped into four larger categories that describe the general subject area: *Self-analysis, Relationships, Life Stressors and Future Focus.* Each song title, theme and a sample lyric are provided in Table 5.2.

Self-analysis. Students used five of the songs on the album as an opportunity for self-analysis, where they engaged in introspective lyric writing toward development. On their song Memories, students looked back at formative moments in their life that impacted their trajectory. To chorus for this song captures this theme well, where students rapped, *"My mind stays black and my head stays scratched, all these thoughts are memories coming back. /Memories that I have, Memories of the past./Memories when we cried and memories when we laughed."* As opposed to Memories (which focused on a range of emotions) students also explored negative life experiences with a song titled Struggle with My Past. With this song the chorus describes the impact of past obstacles and a wish to leave struggle behind – *"I used to struggle with my past, I used to think that life was trash,/I used to struggle with my past, this time I'm gon make it last".* Another song, titled Reminisce, was very similar in nature, using a different beat to engage in the same process of critiquing past experiences toward development – *"stayed strong on them lonely nights, they blockade my way to light,/ upgrade yea I might, dark thoughts to the holy light."* Chains was a song wherein students considered personal thoughts, feelings and

Table 5.2 Adolescent Mixtape Tracklist by Title, Category and Theme.

Song Titles	Song Themes
Self-Analysis (category)	
Memories	Reflecting on formative memories
Struggle with My Past	Overcoming
Reminisce	Introspection
Chains	Feeling held back
One Line	Insecurities
Life Stressors (category)	
Many Men	Navigating threats
Cameras	Documenting police brutality
No Freedom	Disbelief in government
What's Smart	Redefining intellect
Relationships (category)	
You Make it Worse	Family issues
Wonder Why	Tensions in peer relationships
Future Focus (category)	
Live and Prosper	Longevity
Second Chapter	Envisioning the future
Whatchu Mean	Clarifying goals
I Am The Greatest	Confidence
What a Year	Celebrating accomplishments

interactions they felt were holding them back. For example one student wrote, *"I got a lot of learning/These lessons of life too precious I'm earning/Gotta learn how to take care of myself/Need to stop worrying about everybody else"*. Additionally, on their song One Line student's processed specific inse-curities that have hindered their development. A powerful line that highlights this theme was:

> "My insecurities are heavy, dealing with my problems and it's going on so many./
> I was bullied in the past, always got called names like I'm ugly or I'm trash./
> But they didn't know the real me, I was focused on school just try-ing to be a Queen./
> Put problems to the side forget all the lies/
> Show momma that I can and I'm trying not to cry./
> It messes me up mentally, just trying to figure out what I'm meant to be."

Life Stressors. An additional four songs on the Adolescent Mixtape explored life stressors students experienced. One song on the mixtape, Many Men, contained lyrics that detailed feeling the need to fight to survive in an environment – *"Many men don't make it where I'm from/I'm from the jungle yeah the slums where they play with guns./City where it's rough gotta get you some, chase a bag a cash ya check you gotta stack ya funds."* Discussing the stressor of police brutality within their communities and on the news, students wrote Cameras, about their power to use phones to document injustice. One student rapped from the perspective of the camera lens, rhyming,

> "I'm the circle that's attached to the back of ya phone, back in the zone./You won't see violence unless I capture it on/devised lies wouldn't be known unless I show the bare movements/focus on the hand movements."

Continuing the analysis of structural stressors, students wrote a song exploring political issues, titled No Freedom. The lyrics on this song dis-sected how policy creates stressors within the student's communities, such as, *"I want the freedom to do what I want,/I want the freedom to walk freely through the Bronx,/tired of these people dying, tired of the cops lying, tired of the moms crying/...no democracy it's a mockery"*. Through mixtape creation youth shared interest in writing about their struggles feelings successful in a world that fails to value their experiential knowledge. On this track, What's Smart, the chorus details this stressor with lyrics that proclaim, *"What's smart what isn't?/Building up a lie breaking pride in our children. / Numbers are defined that the size of our wisdom, /still got some brothers smarter than my teachers in prison"*.

Relationships. Two songs on the Adolescence project considered family and peer relationships. Family tensions were reflected upon on a song titled, You Make It Worse, where one student specifically performed the following lines: *"I'm the only boy in the fam/You should give me more leeway and just understand. / Why put the pressure all on me try to understand I'm weak, I really don't like it but I'm seriously loving this beat"*. Beyond familial relationships, students processed divides within friend groups with their song, Wonder Why. Questioning the actions of others, one student rhyme *"Wonder why people started changing before the age of 2/ Wonder why people say stuff that don't add up to the truth/Wonder if people hadn't switched up would I still be spitting fire in the booth"*.

Future Focus. The final five songs on the mixtape celebrated accomplishments, explored a sense of confidence and imagined future possibilities. Songs like Live and Prosper contemplated how prior feelings of loss or being trapped allowed for the cultivation of the tenacity to excel,

> "Running through this life, thought it had me trapped then I snapped/ taking straight losses thought I'd never come back,/ that's a fact, now we at the top looking down/they looked down on me but looked what I found."

Similarly, a song called Second Chapter, explored student's beliefs about what they will accomplish despite the opinions of others:

> A better me and better mind is the reason imma blast, boom/
> And it a.in't no question don't make me mention/
> The hours I put in to upgrade the section/Working too hard in the right direction/
> Don't judge me by the light complexion/
> Let god do it in the right selection

Next students clarified the variety of goals they wished to solidify, on a song called Whatchu Mean, which spoke back to people who they felt did not believe in them. Specifically, this song contained lyrics like, *"I'm a king got control I pull the strings,/no I don't play with no orchestra,/ I ain't saying I'm better than the majority,/I just wish there was more of me so they can see my vision"*. Feelings of confidence were on full display in a song called, I Am The Greatest where students shared a personal sense of feeling "chosen" to make history with rhymes like, *"You see I wake up every morning and I'm feeling like I'm chosen/hope my words get preserved too cold n frozen/feeling like I'm golden history imposing/if I see them dethroning a throne they gon be owing"*. The final song on the mixtape (What a Year) allowed students to discuss their pride and feelings of accomplishment in their personal growth, exemplified by rapper Jaydot who rhymed:

Last 12 months felt longer than a year/
Perfection in the rear now I see my vision clear/
Realized life too short to feel fear/
Here lies the old me Jaydot sincere/
Keep it true to myself and forget about what I hear/
You ain't in the radius and you ain't coming near.

Mailability of Mixtape Content

Across the 2016–2017 academic school year, two groups of youth (N=12) engaged in separate mixtape-making projects (six students in each group). On the Hoodies Up Mixtape, youth interrogated policing, creating a total of 21 songs that analyzes group into four overarching categories: *Policing, Overcoming Struggle, Impacting Others, Reflecting on Life Experiences.* The adolescent mixtape, which focused on the development youth in their adolescence broadly, contained 16 songs which fit within 4 overarching categories: *Self-analysis, Relationships, Life Stressors and Future Focus.* Within each of the categories a variety of subthemes were explored in individual songs. While some overlap existed with regard to the content created on each mixtape (i.e., both contained songs focusing on policing, as well as reflecting on and navigating struggle), distinctions existed as well. Through the creation of the Hoodies Up Mixtape youth took a deep dive into the intricacies of unjust murders of Black people by police officers and dedicated five tracks to educating others on injustice impacting them and their communities. Conversely, the Adolescence Mixtape focused on life stressors generally (which included a track on policing), relationships and dedicated five songs to considering their futures. This is not to say that one project was better than the other but is intended to showcase the range of emotions students explored with the CCMC.

Given the disproportionately negative impact of policing on the Black community (Hattery & Smith, 2017), it is not surprising that both youth groups experienced and wrote about unjust interactions with police. There is also a demonstrated need for youth to work through life stressors (Sanchez et al., 2013), given the structural inequities that produce disproportionate environmental stressors for Black and Latinx youth (Santiago et al., 2016). Hip-hop also has the propensity to address social justice issues, with mixtapes being a chief mechanism to achieve this end (Ball, 2011). The Hoodies Up mixtape confirms Ball's (2009, 2011) position on the power of mixtapes in hip-hop, as students used their mixtape to speak back against policing and develop the advocacy skills to share knowledge about structural inequity with others. Additionally, hip-hop mixtapes offer individuals a counter-narrative as a means to overcome adversity (as a result of colonialism and imperialism) and to reimagine the future (Ball, 2011), and to present an authentic version of self that transcends stereotypical perceptions forced on youth by oppressive school structures (Emdin, 2016). The Adolescence Mixtape is an exemplar in this regard, as students processed a variety of intrapersonal, interpersonal and environmental stressors that lead to the concretizing of future goals. Ultimately analysis of student's lyrical content supports the conclusion that the CCMC offers a humanistic process in which students can explore issues of importance to them and begin to consider their own solutions.

Implications for CCMC in School Counseling Practice

School counselors are encouraged to use the CCMC in group work process to support students in addressing issues that are of importance to them. Additionally, school counselors looking to reduce feelings of stress, anxiety and depression among their caseloads might find value in using the CCMC. While not explored directly in this chapter, the CCMC can similarly be used in individual counseling work to lay out a series of emotional themes that will populate sessions. School counselors are expected to act as leaders and advocates within the school community (ASCA, 2019; Bryan et al., 2019) who should push for the removal of policies and structures within their builds that are oppressive to students (Emdin, 2016; Love, 2019). A YPAR-oriented process like the CCMC can be used by counselors to research, process and disseminate mixtapes that target oppressive policy and/or structures in school. School counselors are often called upon to lead and promote equity in discipline practices through restorative justice efforts (Sandwick et al., 2019), as well as to respond to crisis like addressing sudden grief within the community (Hannon et al., 2019). Leading a small group through the CCMC process to reflect on incidents within the school community is recommended. If administration is looking to learn more about school culture and climate, school counselors can lead a small sample of students (representative of the larger school community) through the CCMC with the prompt of reflection on the pros and cons of the school community. The mixtape could then be shared with school staff to reflect on changes they indent to make to respond to student's thoughts and feelings.

Conclusion

Overall, the CCMC is a student-centered, culturally responsive and flexible group counseling process that school counselors can use to support student development. This chapter offered support of this claim, by detailing a theoretical framework for a mixtape-based group process that has mixed methods empirical support evidencing its positive impact on student well-being outcomes and on the range of emotions that students willingly discuss in session. To further support the group counseling process, chapter 6 examines the potential for hip-hop cyphers to accelerate the organic development of group cohesion necessary for vulnerability and healing.

References

American School Counselor Association. (2019). *The ASCA national model: A framework for School counseling programs* (4th ed.). Author.

Ball, J. A. (2009). FreeMix radio: The original mixtape radio show: A case study in mixtape "radio" and emancipatory journalism. *Journal of Black Studies, 39,* 614–634.

Ball, J. A. (2011). *I mix what I like! A mixtape manifesto.* Oakland, CA: AK Press.

Berg, M., Coman, E., & Schensul, J. J. (2009). Youth action research for prevention: A multi-level intervention designed to increase efficacy and empowerment among urban youth. *American Journal of Community Psychology, 43,* 345–359. doi:10.1007/s10464-009-9231-2

Bryan, J., Griffin, D., Kim, J., Griffin, D. M., & Young, A. (2019). School counselor leadership in school family-community partnerships: An equity-focused partnership process model for moving the field forward. In Sheldon, S.B., & Turner-Vorbeck, T.A. (Eds.) *The Wiley handbook on family, school, and community relationships in education,* 265–287. John Wiley & Sons.

Cammarota, J. & Fine, M. (2008). Youth participatory action research. In J. Cammarota & M. Fine (Eds.), *Revolutionizing education* (pp. 1–12). New York: Routledge.

Cook, A. L., & Krueger-Henney, P. (2017). Group work that examines systems of power with young people: Youth participatory action research. *Journal for Specialists in Group Work, 2,* 1–18. doi:10.1080/01933922.2017.1282570

Chen, M. W., & Rybak, C. (2017). *Group leadership skills: Interpersonal process in group counseling and therapy.* SAGE Publications.

Creswell, J. W. (2013). *Qualitative inquiry and research design: Choosing among five approaches.* Los Angeles, CA: Sage.

Del Vecchio, D., Toomey, N., & Tuck, E. (2017). Placing photovoice: Participatory action research with undocumented migrant youth in the Hudson valley. *Critical Questions in Education, 8*(4), 358–376.

Elo, S., & Kyngäs, H. (2008). The qualitative content analysis process. *Journal of Advanced Nursing, 62*(1), 107–115. doi: 10.1111/j.1365-2648.2007.04569

Emdin, C. (2016). *For White folks who teach in the hood... and the rest of y'all too: Reality pedagogy and urban education.* Beacon Press.

Gladding, S. T. (2019). *Groups: A counseling specialty.* Pearson.

Hannon, M. D., Mohabir, R. K., Cleveland, R. E., & Hunt, B. (2019). School counselors, multiple student deaths, and grief: A narrative inquiry. *Journal of Counseling & Development, 97*(1), 43–52.

Hattery, A. J., & Smith, E. (2017). *Policing black bodies: How black lives are surveilled and how to work for change.* Rowman & Littlefield.

Hipolito-Delgado, C. P., & Lee, C. C. (2007). Empowerment theory for the professional school counselor : A manifesto for what really matters. *Professional School Counseling, 10,* 327–332. doi:10.5330/prsc.10.4fm1547261m80x744

Hogg, M. A., & Adelman, J. (2013). Uncertainty–identity theory: Extreme groups, radical behavior, and authoritarian leadership. *Journal of Social Issues, 69*(3), 436–454. doi:10.1111/josi.12023

Jennings, L. B., Parra-Medina, D. M., Hilfinger-Messias, D. K., & McLoughlin, K. (2006). Toward a critical social theory of youth empowerment. *Journal of Community Practice, 14*, 31–55. doi:10.1300/J125v14n01_03

Kohfeldt, D., Chhun, L., Grace, S., & Langhout, R. D. (2011). Youth empowerment in context: Exploring tensions in school-based yPAR. *American Journal of Community Psychology, 47*, 28–45. doi:10.1007/s10464-010-9376-z

Levy, I. (2019). Hip-hop and spoken word therapy in urban school counseling. *Professional School Counseling, 22*(1b), 2156759X19834436.

Levy, I., Emdin, C., & Adjapong, E. S. (2018). Hip-hop cypher in group work. *Social Work with Groups, 41*(1–2), 103–110. https://doi.org/10.1080/01609513.2016.1275265

Levy, I, & Travis, R. (2020). The critical cycle of mixtape creation: Reducing stress via three different group counseling styles. *Journal for Specialists in Group Work, 45*(4), 307–330. doi: 10.1080/01933922.2020.1826614

Love, B. (2019). *We want to do more than survive: Abolitionist teaching and the pursuit of educational freedom.* Beacon Press.

Milsom, A. (2018). Leading groups. In B. Erford (Ed.), *Group work: Processes and applications* (pp. 86–111), Routledge.

Ozer, E. J., & Wright, D. (2012). Beyond school spirit: The effects of youth-led participatory action research in two urban high schools. *Journal of Research on Adolescence, 22*, 267–283. doi:10.1111/j.1532-7795.2012.00780.x

Petchauer, E. (2009). Framing and reviewing hip-hop educational research. *Review of Educational Research, 79*(2), 946–978.

Pulley, B. (2010). *Music industry: How rappers boost street cred.* Bloomberg Businessweek. http://www.businessweek.com/magazine/content/10_25/b4183019425527.htm

Rose, C. (2018). Toward a critical hip-hop pedagogy for teacher education. In C. Emdin & E. Adjapong (Ed). *#HipHopEd: A compilation on hip-hop in education vol 1* (pp. 27–43). Rotterdam: Sense Publishers.

Sanchez, Y. M., Lambert, S. F., & Cooley-Strickland, M. (2013). Adverse life events, coping and internalizing and externalizing behaviors in urban African American youth. *Journal of Child and Family Studies, 22*(1), 38–47. doi: 10.1007/s10826-012-9590-4

Sandwick, T., Hahn, J. W., & Hassoun Ayoub, L. (2019). Fostering community, sharing power: Lessons for building restorative justice school cultures. *Education Policy Analysis Archives, 27*(145), 1–31.

Santiago, C. D., Brewer, S. K., Fuller, A. K., Torres, S. A., Papadakis, J. L., & Ros, A. M. (2016). Stress, coping, and mood among Latino adolescents: A daily diary study. *Journal of Research on Adolescence, 27*(3) 566–580. doi: 10.1111/jora.12294

Singh, A. A., Merchant, N., Skudrzyk, B., & Ingene, D. (2012). Association for specialists in group work: Multicultural and social justice competence principles for group workers. *The Journal for Specialists in Group Work, 37*, 312–325. doi:10.1080/01933922.2012.721482

Sink, C. A., Edwards, C., & Eppler, C. (2011). *School based group counseling.* Cengage Learning.

Smith, L., Beck, K., Bernstein, E., & Dashtguard, P. (2014). Youth participatory action research and school counseling practice: A school-wide framework for student well-being. *Journal of School Counseling, 12*(21), 12–20. Retrieved from http://search.ebscohost.com/login.aspx?direct=true&db=eric&AN=EJ1034747&site=ehost-live

Smith, L., Davis, K., & Bhowmik, M. (2010). Youth participatory action research groups as school counseling interventions. *Professional School Counseling, 14*, 174–182. doi:10.5330/prsc.14.2m62r11337332gt54

Wilson, N., Minkler, M., Dasho, S., Wallerstein, N., & Martin, A. C. (2008). Getting to social action: The Youth Empowerment Strategies (YES!) project. *Health Promotion Practice, 9*, 395–403. doi:10.1177/1524839906289072

Yalom, I., & Leszcz, M. (2005). *The theory and practice of group psychotherapy* (5th ed.). New York, NY: Basic.

6 Hip-Hop Cyphers as Community-Defined Practice to Advance Group Work

Hip-Hop Cyphers as Community-Defined Practice to Advance Group Work

"Are we going to start with a Cypher today?" a student asks as they enter my school counseling office for our small-group session. "Sure, let me find a beat" I reply as the student turns to their peers and announces "Cyph up!". The small group of students excitedly arrange themselves in a circle inside the office, bobbing their heads to the beat playing over the computer speakers. I join the circle, mostly because I can't ever miss out on a cypher, a common reaction from a rapper like myself. Our group ritual of a cypher check-in was underway. Our emotional theme from the prior session, for which we were in the middle of creating a song about, was relationships. Between sessions students were tasked with using their lyric journals as a physical place to process the emergence of daily feelings regarding relationships. One by one, organically with no order, students shared out their daily journal entries within the cypher. The sharing was seamless, that type of "group process" we always look for as facilitators. As one student ended their lyrical contribution, it was met with support and validation, and immediately followed by rhymes from another group member. Occasionally a rhyme would resonate with the group deeply enough that we would erupt in celebration, run around the room and quickly form back in a circle so the cypher could continue. I imagine this is why a passerby, who saw a closed door and heard these celebrations, lauded accusations to school administration that we were "just making hip-hop music" instead of counseling, unable to understand the intricacies of a group process that makes room for authentic, and culturally salient, expression.

Much like the other components of HHSWT, the choice to include the cypher as a component of our larger group process was not some genius-creation of mine. This process is essential to hip-hop. In fact, during my early days as a school counselor, I would often travel to the lunchroom to pick students up for a small group. Ironically, I would interrupt a lunchroom cypher, to pull students into a small-group process wedded to a group curriculum that did not reflect hip-hop in any capacity. It is reasonable to question why students often preferred to stay at lunch in the cypher. A bulk of research would problematize Black and Brown youth for their disinterest in going to group counseling, erroneously claiming they have poor mental health seeking behavior (Heerde & Hemphill, 2018), when in reality this resistance is likely reflective of the fact that the group processes we offer in schools do not allow Black and Brown youth to express and process difficult emotions in culturally authentic ways (Ginter et al., 2018). Choosing to respond to the unspoken, but evident, asks from youth, we moved the cypher to the group counseling session. Additionally, as part of the community-partnership work that fell under the purview of my role as a school counselor, we took school trips to local New York City cyphers to share some of our lyrics from group. The cypher transformed my group counseling process, and in this chapter, I will further explore what the cypher offers to its participants.

I posit that the creation of hip-hop cyphers in group counseling spaces enables clients to enact a series of predefined norms for engagement that support emotional expression. These include (a) participants stand in a circle, (b) each member has an opportunity to share, (c) every voice is viewed as equal, (d) participants are praised when they share and (e) support is provided in moments of discomfort (Levy et al., 2018). The hip-hop cypher is used in HHSWT to establish the environment necessary for students to share emotionally laden lyrics with their group members. The utility of hip-hop cyphers in group counseling practice, however, stems from the importance of cyphers as a cathartic outlet at the community level. This chapter illuminates qualitative research from rappers who reflected on their experiences in cyphers.

Historical Context for Cyphers in Education

Arguments for the value of environments like the cypher, as liberative spaces, are not new. Scholars have documented the use of African music as a social and cultural practice designed for collective community building and release (Anku, 2000). In his explanation of African drum circles, Anku (2000) states "While the music seems to emerge from a principle of collective social participation with a high incidence of social interaction, nevertheless, its practitioners have developed a sense of tolerance for certain apparent disparities that may manifest during performance" (p. 2). As much as drum circles are used within African culture as places for socialization, they also create space for folks to build community and work through issues that arise. Furthering this idea, Snow and D'Amico (2010) found that the integration of West African drum circles into their school counseling program in an urban high school resulted in therapeutic benefits for students.

Famed educator and scholar, Paolo Freire (1970) conducted literacy-related research in Sao Paulo, Brazil, where he engaged with marginalized groups of people through their own cultural circles. Freire (2002) suggests individuals naturally stood in circles with a facilitator to "clarify situations or seek action arising from that clarification" (Freire, 2002, p. 42). Circles were designed as community-defined spaces to discuss individual and collective issues, in attempt to develop solutions. In his work Freire (2002) focused on the use of circles to help validate participants' voices and experiences, through engaging with them on their cultural turf. In his work, Freire (1970) also discussed the use of circles to foster *conscientização*, or critical consciousness, recognizing how circles naturally became a place for community members to discuss and form solutions to oppressive societal structures. Drawing from Freire's work, Karvelis (2020) argued that contemporary approaches to youthwork can involve the analysis of hip-hop as a critical text that supports promoting youth's critical consciousness. In alignment with Emdin (2016) position on the inherent brilliance of Black and Brown youth, Karvelis (2020) advocated for modern day use of hip-hop pedagogy to activate youth's critical consciousness and advocacy. Research on circle and critical consciousness together suggests that the formation of community-based circles promote transformative, and culturally defined, environments. Perhaps cyphers can function as modern circles toward similar outcomes.

Group Counseling Process: A Look at Dynamics and Therapeutic Factors

To assess the value of hip-hop cyphers as a circular space that allows for a group counseling process, we first turn to traditional group work research. The use of small groups in school counseling practice is well documented and largely beneficial (Dispenza et al., 2016; Edwards et al., 2014; Goldstein et al., 2015; Marino et al., 2015). This chapter will not question the use of groups, but it will transgress through the theoretical foundations of group work that explain how groups should function to provide said outcomes. Researchers have found that within group counseling, individuals can engage in conversations based on their lived experiences, pinpoint emotional experiences they have in common and troubleshoot solutions (Yalom & Leszcz, 2005). The facilitation of emotion-based conversations in group therapy allows group members to relate to each other and the content in a much different way than they traditionally do. Yalom and Leszcz (2005) explain 11 primary therapeutic factors that must be present for the group process to occur, including instillation of hope, universality, imparting information, altruism, the corrective recapitulation of the primary family group, development of socializing techniques, imitative behavior, interpersonal learning, group cohesiveness, catharsis and existential factors (Yalom & Leszc, 2005). Toseland and Rivas (2012) further discussed the concept of group dynamics, believed essential for group members' personal growth and completion of therapeutic tasks or outcomes, which overlap with many of the positions of Yalom and Leszcz (2005). Attention to the instillation of group dynamics accelerates socioemotional growth and healing through group work (Toseland & Rivas, 2012), inclusive of the following four dimensions: (1) communication and interaction patterns, (2) cohesion, (3) social integration and influence and (4) group culture. In this chapter, data from research study on hip-hop cyphers is explored, which hypothesized that cyphers organically contain the necessary ingredients for successful group counseling. This begins with a theoretical grounding in group dynamics and therapeutic factors.

Communication and Interaction Patterns and Group Cohesion

Communication and interaction patterns in a group includes both verbal and non-verbal communication and implies that each group member will have a different communication style (Toseland & Rivas, 2012), suggesting that this variability in communication patterns and forms of interaction benefit the functionality of the whole group. The most ideal interaction pattern among a group is to be *free floating* – where each member takes responsibility for their own communications, believing in their capacity to provide meaningful information to the group dialogue, and the conversation moves back and forth between all group members seamlessly. As group members communicate and interact, they can impart information on one another regarding their life experiences, such as tools for perseverance, or validating difficulties (Yalom & Leszcz (2005). Group communication and interaction patterns are influenced by the emotional bonds group members develop as they impact the reinforcement individuals receive for interacting (Toseland & Rivas, 2012). Through honest and reflective communication and emotional evocating in group, members can access catharsis (Yalom & Leszcz, 2005).

Group cohesion refers to a combination of how attracted group members are to the group and each other, how unified and connected the group feels, as well as the amount that a group is able to meet its goals (Forsyth, 2010). Kelly and Hunter (2016) state that the more cohesive a group is, the more likely group members are to attend, participate and work toward individual and collective goals. Cohesion also increases the amount of listening and expression of both positive and negative feelings (Corey, 2009). As such Toseland and Rivas (2012) suggest that groups promote affiliation, recognition, security, rewards for participation, feedback and evaluation to make them more attractive to members. Similarly, Yalom and Leszcz (2005) presented the term universality as a therapeutic factor where group members find solace in shared struggles that they may have formerly felt alone in and theorized that group members function as a family group that works through existing familial tensions.

Social Integration, Influence and Culture

Social integration and influence play a large role in the cultivation and sustainment of group cohesion as they refer to how well individual members fit inside of a group, and how group members feel about each other's fit (Toseland & Rivas, 2012). The establishment of norms, roles and the status of each group member defines the impact of social integration and influence. Norms are the "shared expectations and beliefs about appropriate ways to act in a social situation such as a group" (Toseland & Rivas, 2012, p. 82). Roles refer to the functions each member is believed to have within a group and are closely tied to norms. The status of individuals in the group is relative to the amount of prestige or perceived power they have in the group, with higher status individuals controlling a session and lower status individuals confirming to the norms (Toseland & Rivas, 2012). For example, Yalom and Leszcz (2005) describe altruism as a therapeutic factor that occurs when a member raises his or her self-esteem after/by helping someone, learning that the sharing of their own personal struggles can be worth something to others. The therapeutic factor of imitative behavior implies that more novice group members can learn behaviors from more experienced members. Through the practicing and trying of new behaviors, individuals can develop socialization techniques which support addressing increased emotional disclosure and the ability to address conflict in group. The culmination of interactions in groups helps to define the group culture, ideally an environment where a sharing and understanding of each group member's values, beliefs, traditions and customs can occur (Toseland & Rivas, 2012). In fact, "shared life experiences, goals, and purpose, will often expedite the emergence of a group culture" (Kelly & Hunter, 2016, p. 310). A solidified group culture is crucial in bringing a group together but can isolate those who do not identify with it. Group culture, as a group dynamic, evinces the need to deploy approaches to group work that are relevant to the culture of participants.

Assessing the Cultural Complexities of Hip-Hop Cyphers

While my experiences with youth in cyphers are largely anecdotal, my observational knowledge has suggested that many of the group dynamics and therapeutic factors needed for a successful counseling group, naturally existed within hip-hop cyphers. It was my belief, that beyond the context of schooling, hip-hop cyphers offered participants a place for healing because the physical environment allows for emotional discussions and vulnerability. Developing evidence to support this position would aid the use of hip-hop cyphers in group work to create the student experiences I described at the start of this chapter, a group environment that allows for an organic process toward cohesion and healing. Theoretically, HHSWT draws from a deep understanding of community-defined hip-hop practices to inform counseling interventions. So, to assess the value of cyphers in HHSWT praxis, it was necessary to first understand the experiences of hip-hop community members inside of cyphers.

Relevant Methods

This phenomenological study functioned as an analysis of seven rappers' experiences in hip-hop cyphers. In particular the research was interested in exploring the experiences of hip-hop artists to glean implications for the use of cyphers to bolster group dynamics and establish therapeutic factors within counseling groups. Participants in this study were local hip-hop artists in the Northeast, who willingly participated in, individual, over-the-phone interviews. A total of seven rappers volunteered (five male and two female) and ranged between the ages of 18 and 35. The researcher designed nine interview questions about rappers' experiences. One research question guided this inquiry: *What are the experiences of participants in hip-hop cyphers?*

Data Analysis

All interviews were recorded using "Voice Memo" application on an iPhone, and the audio recordings were then transcribed. An interpretative phenomenological analysis (IPA) was used as a data analysis strategy to support the exploration of participants lived experience within their social contexts (Smith et al., 2009). IPA is specifically well positioned as an analysis strategy in this study because it allows for the capturing of participants' subjective explanations of their experiences, by engaging in an in-depth analysis of participants' narratives and context (Pietkiewicz & Smith, 2014). Rather than attempting to identify a frequency at which themes occur, the purpose of IPA is to capture the meaning behind participants' statements. Therefore, each interview transcript was read a number of times to digest the rapper's perspective, followed by a step-by-step process of making meaning of the rapper's experiences. The audio recording of the interview was read to create codes, which were grouped based on their commonalities into short descriptive phrases that constituted lower-order themes. Connections were established for a various grouping of lower-order themes into various, higher-order themes assigned as overarching categories as a way identifying meaning (interpretative analysis).

Results of Interviews with Rappers

Analysis of interviews with rappers resulted in the identification of three higher-order themes, each of which contained a handful of lower-order themes codifying experiences rappers shared in cyphers. The first higher-order theme indicated that within cyphers rappers experienced *valuable communication and interaction.* Five lower order themes that fell within this higher-order theme further suggesting that rappers experienced *interpersonal communication and relationship building, developing cohesion,* feeling *empowered by competition, conflict and tension resolution* and *spiritual connection.* The second higher-order theme showed rappers experienced *intrapersonal development,* including three lower-order themes of *developing comfort expressing, catharsis* and *personal development.* The final higher-order suggested rappers experienced *navigating norms and roles,* with two lower order themes of *adhering to unspoken rules* and *noticing roles* of the cypher.

Valuable Communication and Interaction

Analysis of interviews revealed that though participating in hip-hop cyphers, rappers experienced valuable communication and interaction. That is, rappers were offered a unique environment that helped them practice and work on interpersonal skills. A total of five lower-order themes define the specific ways in which this interactive and communicative space was deemed valuable, including the cypher offering *interpersonal communication and relationship building, a deeper awareness of others, conflict and tension resolution, and empowerment through competition and spiritual connection.*

Interpersonal Communication and Relationship Building

Reflecting on what felt like to be inside of cyphers, the rappers highlighted the ways in which the cypher supported tangible development of communication skills and relationships. Relationally, we know that strong relationships are established through the sharing and listening to one's authentic lived experiences (Gelso, 2009). A particular quote from an interviewee read, *"there's something that's just innate about that output and I think you learn a lot about a person or people in those settings, how they communicate, how they listen, how they don't."* Participating in cyphers allowed rappers to learn who their peers were, innately, and subsequently how to get them to listen.

The ability to share thoughts and feelings in a way that will resonate with rappers however, required first an interpersonal understanding. Interactions within the cypher enabled rappers to feel a sense of familiarity with their peers. One rapper stated this directly, saying, *"once you get more familiar with people you know what to expect and so you get more in tune with them"*. By feeling in tune with others in the cypher, rappers are confident they will be listened to and able to communicate the complexities of their lived experiences with their peers. So, when rappers share quotes like *"I think the reason why it was so dope for me and it made me want to jump in because it's constant confirmation. When I say something dope and then everybody goes, "Ooooh," Oh, okay, so I got something here"* they are noting that communication is not unidirectional. When a rapper shares, they receive feedback indicating that their peers were listening and that their words resonated, ultimately enabling rappers to feel validated and connected to their peers. Communication breeds relationships in cyphers.

Developing Cohesion

As rappers learn to communicate and build relationships with one another, results evidenced that these interactions might culminate in the cypher's cohesiveness. Whereas the communication rappers experienced reinforced the receipt of feedback during interactions, cohesiveness is the result of unity and connectedness which support collaboratively moving forward (Forsyth, 2010). Quotes from rappers indicated that cyphers themselves could deepen relationships to the extent that rappers understood the subtleties of their peer's behavior and even adopted some of those tendencies toward a unified whole. One rapper commented:

> "Eventually you get to a point where stylistically their style begins to influence your style. And your style begins to influence their style. You start to notice subtleties, and cadences, it becomes more complementary to one-another over time."

The growth in connectedness that rappers experience was further evident in statements like:

> "Rappin with a certain person so many times, you gotta figure out how that begins to mesh together. There's an evolution where like, you go in here and we all sound a little different but as we grow together, rap together, we began to develop things that were more complementary and intentionally started playing off each other."

Cohesion within cyphers looks and sounds like rappers intentionally figuring out how to "mesh together" in order to collectively evolve and grow.

The intentionality behind the establishment of cohesion, however, cannot be overlooked. Rappers are not grabbing onto any style or behavior within the cypher, they are working with each other to explore and decide on the best path forward. A particular quote highlights the intricacies in the development of cohesion:

> "If I know them, I know what their skillsets are, I know what colors are in their rhyme palates, I have a sense of where their comfort zone is, what their norms are, and how to push or pull that, and also an understanding of how willing to flex with me they may or may not be."

Through a knowledge of their peer's communication styles, skillsets and personality, rappers learn how to push each other toward a collective whole. Since building together toward cohesion requires learning to blend different styles, ideas and behaviors, rappers intentionally decide how to best corral group members around group goals.

Empowered by Competition

Establishing cohesiveness in a cypher is empowering for many rappers. Various quotes credit the competitive nature of cyphers for supporting the exploration of new styles, ideas and behaviors to find out how to fit within the group. For example, a rapper mentioned:

> "I get really excited when I hear somebody do something like really dope and it kind of makes me want to match it, but at the same time try to have the etiquette to like fall back and allow folks to do that and then come in when appropriate."

While there is a distinct urge to want to match your peers in the cypher, learning how to do this appropriately is paramount. Regardless, an urge to prove oneself within the cypher can support rappers in showing others who they are, and what they bring to the collective. The following quote reads:

> "Sometimes it lights a fire under you to be in front of complete strangers. It's more exciting for them because they have no idea what to expect when you walk into a cypher and they are just pinning you one way or another, judging you before things even come out of your mouth. That's a great feeling, to be able to surprise people."

This statement indicates that competition plays a key role in the development of individuality. While judgment might be perceived as something that is negative, here it actually functions as an invite to show others who you are. The dynamic of competition can empower those who are either ambivalent about sharing, or publicly perceived as quiet or shy, to share. This phenomenon is further evidenced by the following quote:

> "I've come off unassuming most of the time in my history. I like waiting patiently to go off and have people like 'oh okay, all right'. I like that feeling, I'm not going to lie. It's fun to hop into cyphers with people that I don't know just to show myself off."

Overall, there is a level of empowerment that comes with disproving people's perceptions. The competitive atmosphere in the cypher teaches participants how to advocate for their voice.

Resolving Conflict and Tension

Rappers also agreed that a good amount of tension can manifest in cyphers. However, this tension was often successfully navigated for the betterment of the group. Conflict and tension occurred for a number of reasons, all seemingly rooted in the group working toward establishing a collective. Discussing a particularly tense moment, one rapper shared:

> "I've been the dude to cut somebody off. It didn't turn into an altercation per se, but there were definitely some words exchanged and it was all peace at the end of the day. But it was with like a younger kid who felt slighted by this, and it's just like, 'no, this is what you jumped into.'"

As previously mentioned, competition in the cypher often involves proving your voice, while being careful to adhere to cypher etiquette. In the above example, a rapper accidently cut someone off but was able to resolve the situation. Instead of feeling shame or regret about causing turbulence, the rapper confirmed that tension is an expected part of the cypher. Other rappers name tension as a result of being disrespected:

> "Tension comes from a place of being disrespected, but it is all pounds and smiles at the end. It's a place where I think catharsis can exist in terms of working through tension and anger together and doing so non-violently from a place of humor based navigation."

Quite similarly, tension is explained as resolved through "pounds" (fist-bumps or handshakes), or smiles. However, the emotional process of tension transcends the pound and provides a healthy environment to non-violently work together to reach cohesion.

In other instances, tension emerged through the sharing of content that upset group members. Reflections on how to address uncomfortable content were discussed in interviews:

> "Cyphers can be very thought provoking because people will drop knowledge about different things that maybe you didn't know before. The issues of homophobia and misogyny always come up in hip-hop as far as the discussion around it. I may want to check them. Sometimes I do, sometimes I don't. But I have to gauge the situation because I have an understanding of why you're rapping like this. I don't want to come at your neck but I still want you to be thoughtful about what you're saying."

The beauty of the cypher is that it enables the authentic sharing of one's thoughts and feelings which, as the quote above indicates, can allow participants to adopt new knowledge. However, occasionally harmful comments (misogyny or homophobia) might be made that create discomfort. This tension appears to also be navigated in a non-violent and conversational manner in which rappers figure out how to understand the positions of others while also holding them accountable. When exploring the results around cohesion, rappers were intentional about how groups formed a collective. This quote exemplifies the intentional process of using conflict to hold group members accountable and form a safe, comfortable and cohesive environment.

Spiritual Connection

The establishment of interpersonal communication and relationship building, cohesion, empowering competition and the resolution of conflict and tension created what rappers consistently named as an *energy* they felt in the cypher. The rappers believed that entering cyphers was less about their individual performance, and more about collectively joining something that was bigger than themselves. This energy was exciting and allowed for individual creative expression, but ultimately, the creation of a group space that was beyond the individual. The following quote names this connection:

> "It's just that collective energy of, it feels like real spiritual you know what I'm saying? Like people going to church or having a religious experience. Man, it's that same level when people get to go in and they can just feed off other people and um then it's just going back and forth and everything is getting better, and better, and you know the beats getting better and we're playing off of each other."

In this quote, the rapper highlighted a ubiquitous experience for cypher participants, a feeling of excitement stemming from building each other up and establishing a strong unit. Another rapper suggested that through spiritual connection the cypher allowed members to see raw and authentic presentations of others:

> "I think there's a sense of community to it that I think is really important. You get an interesting sense of somebody when you're going just off the head with them. There's a side of somebody that you see that I don't think that they, it's a very raw, natural side when someone's just moving through something whether it be content, speech, rhythm."

The cypher helped participants find a community who they felt deeply connected with.

Rappers further attributed individual's contributions to the cypher as supportive of the spiritual connection they experienced. Specifically, a rapper commented:

> "like the energy of cypher. I like hearing people's perspective on life. I like hearing dope literature; like the wordplay and different thoughts and creativeness that people bring. That stuff is so dope and I like to be around that energy as well as it being a space for me to go in there and do my thing as well."

From sharing individual perspectives on life, to sharing their wordplay, thought processes or creativeness, rappers felt that a specific energy had been established that supported collective advancement. Individually rappers were able to be themselves, but this is because they functioned as pieces of a larger picture. The confluence of rapper's experiences with the energy of the cypher promoted a feeling that they were there for something bigger than themselves, a community that they were thankful to have.

Intrapersonal Development

Beyond results that substantiate the interactional benefits of the hip-hop cypher, rappers noted the *intrapersonal development* they experienced through their participation. Three emergent lower-order themes serve as descriptive evidence to illuminate the ways in which interpersonal growth was experienced, including *comfort exploring self, catharsis* and *personal growth*. Examples of quotes that fit within each of these lower-order themes are listed below.

Comfort Exploring Self

When reflecting on what drew them to cyphers, rappers named a newfound comfort exploring themselves. Self-exploration, or the process of finding oneself, is closely linked with finding one's place within a social group (Cantor et al., 2002). Quotes from rappers illuminated that cyphers, as a social group, enabled participants to uncover parts of themselves, such as:

> "I think it allows you to tap into certain parts of yourself that may not be on the surface and allow you to deal with them, but before you can actually deal with anything, you have to be aware of it. Otherwise you're just taking shots in the dark."

As a prerequisite to healing, rappers claimed that cyphers enable the evocation of emotions or parts of self that can subsequently be dealt with. This self-discover is only possible if there is a willingness to express, which rappers identify as necessary for participation in cyphers:

> "Being open is the best thing I can always hope for in any type of freestyle situation. When you're just a conduit for whatever is coming through you and going out to the world. I think that comfort level, and a level of familiarity promotes that, because you're not trying to impress, you're not preconceiving of what you're going to say too much."

This comfort emoting that participants identified is different from when rappers attempt to prove themselves in the cypher. Comfort level or feeling familiar with expressing, without the need to impress others, allows one to be a conduit for an authentic freestyle (making up rhymes on the spot) or a free-flow of thoughts and feelings. Embracing a readiness to openly express and explore self requires vulnerability, or as one rapper put it, *"Man I would say, I've felt nervous. The good nervous, the adrenaline that comes from, like I said, knowing that you're about to do something that is beyond yourself"*. In sum, exploring aspects of one's identity that are considered "beyond" current consciousness requires comfort, openness, the removal of ego and vulnerability, which are attainable in the cypher.

Catharsis

The impact of the hip-hop cypher on participants' intrapersonal development does not end at self-exploration. In fact, the rapper's quotes help support the conclusion that comfort evocating parts of self is the first step toward catharsis, release or healing. The potential relationship between comfort expressing and catharsis is detailed in the following quote:

> "When you get over that hump, when you master that fright, when you master that, what is on the other side is just phenomenal. It's

an outer-body experience, I mean I've just blacked out in cyphers. Now that feeling, you know that outer-body, is such a release."

Tapping into previously unassessed parts of oneself, in an authentic and unplanned capacity, can generate a feeling of release for rappers in cyphers. Rappers discussed the emergence of feelings and subsequent processing, in quotes like:

> "I feel like the catharsis is you get to exercise these demons and be proud of yourself for being able to do it rhythmically and musically in a crowd of people at the same time. That's a beautiful fusion of feelings. At the same time you know that these people are feeling what you saying. It's a very immense cathartic feeling that I've had before in the cypher."

Building on the interpersonal dynamics assessed earlier, participants learned to listen to and respect each other as part of the cypher. On an individualized level, the communication, relationships and cohesion allow rappers to express emotional vulnerabilities and receive validation (catharsis). Catharsis is reached within a cypher not only by expressing but also by hearing other people share their feelings. One quote exemplifies this phenomenon, *"but a cypher, you share with other people. It's not just you, it's everyone involved. That makes everyone feel good. You know like because you hear people sharing that, you hear people sharing this."* Through listening to their peers, rappers can access release and healing.

Personal Growth

Having access to a physical space where an array of authentic feelings can come to the surface resulted in rappers reporting that cyphers fostered personal growth. Rappers identified an array of personal growths, with statements suggesting that cyphers *"largely taught me how to rap, how to think quickly, how to listen, how to advocate for myself. I've learned as much rapping in the cypher as I have by observing and listening. It's taught me humility"*. Personal growth areas like quick thinking, listening and self-advocacy resulted in a learned humility. Analysis of interviews with rappers also found that cyphers helped build self-confidence. A particular quote notes this development:

> "I was kind of obscure before I started rhyming so entering in a cyphers got me like props, got me credit. Like, 'Ok, who is this guy? What's his name? Where's he from? What's he doing?' Uh, just a place to shine. So first I would probably say confidence building."

On an interpersonal level cyphers contain a competitive atmosphere that empowers rappers to prove themselves through lyrical expression.

An outcome of competition for airtime might be that rappers feel more confident. In the above quote a rapper displays a sense of pride in finding a way to shine within cyphers, to show others that he had something worthy of props, which he felt increased his confidence.

Other personal development outcomes are highlighted in a rapper quote that reads, *"I have learned to get along with people from all walks of life. It's a very egalitarian place once you enter the cypher. I've learned about crews and who will have your back and conflict resolution"*. This statement communicates that rappers can learn empathy and compassion for people from all walks of life, as well as how to identify support systems and to navigate tension. Perhaps not dissimilar from the interpersonal components of the cypher that rappers spoke of, where conflict resolution and relationship building happened, but the quotes in this lower-order theme give us a direct glimpse impact of group dynamics on individual development.

Navigating Norms and Roles

Distinct from the interpersonal dynamics, and the ways in which rappers garnered personal development, were comments that offered insight into the structural functionality of the cypher. While participating in cyphers, rappers experienced *navigating norms and roles*. This third higher-order theme contained two lower-order themes wherein rappers spoke about *adhering to unspoken norms* and *noticing roles* that existed within the cypher.

Adhering to Unspoken Norms

When commenting on how cyphers were maintained or organized, participants noted a specific set of norms that governed the space. Each participant who was interviewed mentioned these norms, as well as the fact that no one had named these norms to them specifically. For example, a number of norms were covered in the following quote:

> "If someone raps you at least let them get 8 bars in, which is an unspoken rule that you have to protect. And it's not like being dominant, you just can't be quiet, or people will rap over you. You'd think that be a rule not to rap over people but it's like the opposite. If you're being rapped over your gonna have to back off or rap harder."

From this quote we learn that everyone who shares should be allowed to rhyme for at least eight bars (or measures) and that this amount of airtime is protected for everyone. Additionally, you have to learn how to insert yourself so you are not rapped over, which will not be perceived as mean-spirited but, in fact, appreciated. This "insert yourself" norm is similar to the competitive nature of the cypher dynamics mentioned earlier, it is a norm that helps ensure everyone has a chance to be heard. Similarly, if a person is sharing and is doing particularly well, participants must let that individual continue. This rule was directly articulated by a rapper who said:

> "There are no rules to the cypher written down anywhere, I think most of the rules that I bring to a cypher, and hope people have come from a place of self-awareness. This from a jazz school of thought, or what I would interpret to be a jazz of thought. When you're on fire, it's amazing, and if you have a good sense of when that is, and can read it in other people, and allow that to flourish, that's great."

It is the responsibility of rappers within a cypher to notice when someone is particularly locked-in, with regard to their sharing, and to help them flourish.

The next norm, like those before it, has not been written down anywhere, it was just learned. This norm pertained to the proximity of participants to each other in the cypher:

> "There are rules about the distance you keep, and when you come in with your verse, and not to go extra-long, and not to go extra short because a person is still kinda workin out what they're saying. And then to not be trying to hog the mic. Like, that's not the feel that we're doing right now. Those seem to just be unwritten rules, I don't remember anyone telling me those things, I just grew up where it was going down like that."

The norms of the cypher appear to be learned experientially. There is also an implied balancing of how long you allow people to rap for within cyphers. You want to let individuals shine when they are locked-in, but not hog the mic. At the same time everyone should have a chance to share at least eight bars, but not go too short because they might force the next person to jump in before they are ready to do so. It is incredible that each of these norms are navigated non-verbally. This might be because of the reality that so many rappers are good at listening and understanding each other within the cypher. A final quote from a rapper highlights listening as a norm, *"As much as it's about speaking, rhyming and rapping, I think the cypher is more about listening. You really have to be paying attention and I think that's how you can tell in a cypher who's more seasoned than not."*

Noticing Roles

As a final lower-order theme, rappers experienced noticing the roles that individuals within the cypher play that help it function. One rapper noticed that roles occurred naturally within the cypher, saying that

"I think those roles come up organically. I try to be the responsible uncle in cypher sometimes. I'll take that position of if I feel like there's homophobia going crazy I'll be like yo chill. If misogyny is going crazy I'll be like yo chill but I won't say it in an aggressive manner."

As evidenced by this quote, members might confront each other if they feel that inappropriate content is shared. The emergence of difficult content within the cypher is handled by the group itself, as a means to ensure feelings of comfort and safety and to allow group members a chance to become more thoughtful about what they are saying. Aside from playing the role of a content curator of sorts, rappers spoke about "leaders" within cyphers:

"You can model leadership in ways. If you see someone like cut someone off and is going on and on and on, then you can kind of help just with like two or four bars just intervene and get it back to that other person."

In support of adhering to the airtime norm, leaders might step in when a given member is not allowed their full eight bars of sharing. Leaders support others in the cypher, in-part, by helping them access enough time to express. When these roles emerge however, they are not pre-defined. One rapper explained that roles are selected by individuals in relation to their specific skillsets:

"People develop roles who has what strong suits in terms what they can contribute. And those things can but in some kind of organic but repeatable arrangement of distribution of different types of things. Some people are good rapping others are good singing or making noises, sounds or dancing, or OGs that just keep people on task."

So, whether one has singing, rapping or dancing skills they organically find a way to use or perform a role that accentuates the cypher. Additionally, OGs (older members with credibility and status) exist to keep participants on-task within the cypher.

Uses of Cyphers in Group Work

This particular study sought to understand the experiences of rappers who participate in hip-hop cyphers. Results indicated broadly that rappers experienced valuable communication and interaction (including *interpersonal communication and relationship building, developing cohesion, empowerment by competition, conflict and tension resolution and spiritual connection)*, intrapersonal development (including *developing comfort expressing, catharsis and personal growth)* and navigating norms and roles (including *adhering to unspoken rules* and *noticing roles)*. A salient aspect of the HHSWT is the coupling of community-defined hip-hop practices with counseling theory, in order to elevate the counseling process. Analysis of interviews with rappers revealed a medley of ways in which cyphers contain the very dynamics and therapeutic factors we hope to foster in counseling groups. Additionally, there are a number of implications for how cyphers can be used in small-group counseling praxis to offer youth a culturally responsive and authentic group counseling process. In this final section I will discuss higher- and lower-order theme within the context of group dynamics and therapeutic factors, and then extrapolate their value for school counselors who facilitate small groups.

Valuable Communication and Interaction: Connections to Group Theory

In an ideally functioning group process, communication and interaction between group members should benefit the whole group, enabling a free-flowing conversation where members learn to relate to each other, believe in the value of their contributions, discuss emotional experiences, validate each other's feelings and build emotional bonds (Toseland & Rivas, 2012; Yalom & Leszcz, 2005). Although hip-hop cyphers are not defined as group counseling spaces by school counselors, rappers in the current study reported they learned about the intricacies of peers, how they listened and how to share content that resonates with others. Generally, their interactions and communications within the cypher left rappers feeling validated, authentically heard and connected with peers.

As rappers participated in cyphers, they learned to blend different styles, ideas and behaviors together to create a unified whole. Additionally, rappers learned about individual differences between group members, their particular expression styles and were able to adopt new behaviors to create cyphers that collectively worked towards goals. The interactional experiences reported by rappers are synonymous with the establishment of group cohesion, described as a unified and connected group (Forsyth, 2010) where members actively attend, participate and work toward individual and collective goals (Kelly & Hunter, 2016). Like the reports from rappers, cohesive groups offer participants a space to practice and try out new behaviors; individuals can develop socialization techniques which support individual and collective emotional disclosure and growth (Yalom & Leszcz, 2005).

Two additional benefits to groups are that they help individuals address and work through conflict and offer novice members a chance to learn helpful behaviors from more experienced members (Yalom &

Leszcz, 2005). The current study confirms that hip-hop cyphers can offer participants opportunities for conflict resolution and that they provide a competitive atmosphere that pushes members to match each other's skills to create a unified whole. The competitive nature of cyphers further supported rappers in proving their individual value, learning to try new styles to express themselves in a way that resonated with their peers. Not all groups are able to reach a place where they are comfortable enough to work through tension (the storming stage), particularity in a way that ends with smiles, compassion and understanding (Bonebright, 2010). The fact that cyphers as groups promote storming is notable, as this may reveal a valuable and culturally relevant tactic to develop cohesion in groups.

Participants also named cyphers as places where they collectively gathered to create something bigger than themselves, akin to that of a spiritual connection. Durkheim (1912) introduced the term collective effervescence to separate daily mundane activities from those of special significance that produce a level of emotional excitement that allows groups of individuals a high level of energy described as sacred. More modern interpretations from Gabriel et al. (2020) espouse that collective effervescence can occur through a "small and/or common collective gathering that may give meaning, a sense of connection, and joy to life" and enable a "powerful psychological experience connected to strong emotions and wellbeing" (p. 129). It appears that, organically, hip-hop cypher's generate collective effervescence, or the establishment of group dynamics and therapeutic factors necessary for psychological growth.

Practical Implications

The possible use of cyphers in small-group counseling practice feels limitless. For starters, youth should be encouraged to share out their emotionally laden rhymes through the cypher. This type of sharing, if consistently used, can support youth in developing interpersonal communication skills as well as stronger relationships with group members. There is also evidence that cyphers can be used in group work toward cohesion and individuality in that group members will organically find ways to both listen to and validate each other's lived experiences. Evidence supports that cyphers are bigger than the individual, and their use in middle or high schools can offer a culturally organic and relevant medium for youth to establish a collective, and even spiritual, space to work toward co-defined goals. Students who are shy and need to learn new mediums for expression can safely learn from more experience members in cyphers, given their competitive and empowering nature. Lastly, cyphers can be used for the express purpose of navigating conflict and tension between group members, with individuals within the school, or to address familial divides.

Intrapersonal Development: Connections to Group Theory

One of the hallmarks of effective counseling groups are that participants feel a sense of safety and comfort with vulnerable self-expression (Yalom & Leszcz, 2005). Drawing from a humanistic frame, a group facilitator would believe they are doing their job optimally when they are almost entirely removed from the process and the clients have a free-flowing conversation in which they uncover their internalized solutions to their own concerns (Glassman, 2008). A great deal of play or activity-based therapies pull from this reality, offering an experiential exercise that helps clients talk freely and uncover subconscious thoughts and feelings, which the facilitator then highlights to bring to conscious awareness (Kottman, & Meany-Walen, 2016). The current study concluded that cyphers provided rappers with the sense of comfort and relational familiarity necessary to emote and tap into their subconscious. Rappers explained that the cypher facilitated them reaching a place that was beyond themselves, where they "blacked out" as they expressed feelings. There appears to be great utility in cyphers to help individuals tap into their subconscious, to uncover thoughts and feelings that can then be highlighted and explored in session.

Through vulnerability and free-flowing self-expression rappers reported feeling a sense of catharsis. That is, when emotional vulnerabilities were expressed, they were validated. Yalom and Leszcz (2005) confirm that catharsis is the result of honest and reflective communication and emotional evocating in group, often supported by universality. However, catharsis and emotional evocation were made available via an authentic community-defined practice that promotes group members' ability to generate the answers to their own and collective emotion concerns. Through emoting in the cypher, rappers learned to think quickly, listen critically and with empathy and compassion, self-advocate, and feel increased pride and self-confidence. Each of these outcomes is deemed necessary for adolescent development in schools (ASCA, 2019).

Practical Implications

Within school counseling, small-groups are used to support developing empathy and compassion, listening to and considering the perceptive of others and to increase self-esteem and self-advocacy (ASCA, 2019). Oftentimes this work is done assuming youth lack said skills and then placing them in small-groups as an intervention to mediate this deficit (ASCA, 2019), which runs counter to Emdin's (2016) position that education is used to denounce or erase Black and Brown youth's inherent knowledge. However, what is implied by this study is that if we help to create group environments that enable youth to use community-defined practices and their own cultural knowledge to support the expression and discussion of emotions, we will see youth express the very skills they are wrongfully believed to lack. Much like prior research that found hip-hop mixtapes a valuable group counseling process for youth to engage in action research and challenge systemic inequities (Levy et al., 2018), the use of cyphers supports the belief that youth have all of the skills needed to express and sort through emotions for individual and collective development. It is the responsibility of school counselors to understand the importance of integrating hip-hop cyphers into their group work to directly challenge traditional group counseling approaches which not only lack cultural relevance, but are used to minimize the experiences, knowledge, skills and brilliance of Black and Brown youth.

Navigating Norms and Roles: Connections to Group Theory

In counseling groups, norms govern the shared expectations and behaviors that group members follow (Toseland & Rivas, 2012). In practice, particularly with adolescence, norms are established through a discussion with the group during the first week. Norm setting is often presented as serious process, which must be upheld by all group members. Norms are defined early on as they are believed to be essential in supporting participants in accessing a sense of comfort and belonging needed for growth (Gladding, 2015). For example, facilitators want to be sure that participants all have equal airtime and that no one monopolizes the space verbally (Chu & Kendall, 2004). In the current study however, we saw that cyphers contained a set of unspoken norms that rappers learned over time. Almost effortlessly, the rappers explained how airtime was navigated, how to understand and support someone who is locked into a pivotal moment of sharing and how to learn to actively listen to what was happening within the cypher. The organic establishment of norms within the cypher stands in direct opposition to the age-old practice of counselors setting the norms for or with the group. In fact, the rigid constructing of norms might create barriers for the unspoken and organic norms to emerge. Instead, the current study encourages us to let go of those power dynamics (i.e., facilitators rushing to make sure that no one monopolizes, or that everyone upholds the norms) and to trust in the cypher's ability to establish and uphold norms.

There is reason to believe that the norms will be upheld by cypher participants, who naturally fall into roles that help sustain the cypher as a validating, safe and empowering communal space. In the current study, we saw that certain rappers helped create a competitive spirit that encouraged novice rappers' to step in and show their authentic selves. To protect the airtime of participants, some rappers fell into leadership roles wherein they tried to stop people from getting cut off. Others brought innate skills to the cypher, taking on dancing, singing and making noises as their role. Older members with lots of credibility held the role of keeping the group on-task. Much like norms, all roles within the cypher were developed organically, suggesting that the cypher promotes individuals finding out what they specifically bring to the group, and learning to own that role in the collective whole.

Navigating Norms and Roles: Practical Implications

To establish norms within small-groups in schools, the cypher can prove quite helpful. For example, school counselors can have youth reflect on cyphers they've been in and what types of behaviors they like and dislike. Through this discussion the facilitator can pull out norms for the group to agree upon. Alternatively, a facilitator might have students write a short introductory 4-bar verse and share it within a cypher. Given what we know about cyphers, we can be confident youth will validate each other, maintain a circular space, refrain from cutting each other off, and critically listen. After the group shares, the facilitator can have students reflect on the process. Asking students "What types of roles did we each play in that cypher?" or "What did people do while someone was sharing?" school counselors can lead a here-and-now reflection on the cypher experience, to then agree upon a shared list of norms. The school counselor's role in the functionality of the cypher is minimal. The community will uphold the norms, rules, and roles, the school counselor might only have to keep the group on task. In fact, the OG role might be easily filled by the facilitator or a more experienced group member who functions as the guiding force (with regards to keeping the group on task, making sure that airtime is respected, and that tension is navigated). The school counselor can keep their distance, only playing a leadership role in the event that they need to. Otherwise, they can trust that the cypher will take care of itself with regard to norms and roles, believing again in youth capacity to find solutions to their own concerns.

Conclusion

This chapter sought to gather knowledge on the experiences of rappers to assess the value of the hip-hop cypher as a group counseling tool. Drawing from experiential knowledge noting the power and potential of cyphers in engaging youth and offering an environment to share difficult thoughts and feelings, I led a series of interviews with rappers to further explore anecdotal conclusions. An analysis of interviews revealed that hip-hop cyphers contain many of the group dynamics and therapeutic factors that traditional literature deems necessary for successful group development and the growth of students, and have implications for school counseling practice. Moreover, this chapter provides strong qualitative support to the use of hip-hop cyphers as a component of

HHSWT. In the following, and final, chapter of this text I will discuss how school counselors can ready themselves to deploy HHSWT comprehensively.

References

American School Counselor Association. (2019). *The ASCA national model: A framework for school counseling programs* (4th ed.) Author.

Anku, W. (2000). Circles and time: A theory of structural organization of rhythm in African music. *Music Theory Online, 6*(1), 1–8.

Bonebright, D. A. (2010). 40 years of storming: a historical review of Tuckman's model of small group development. *Human Resource Development International, 13*(1), 111–120.

Cantor, N., Kemmelmeier, M., Basten, J., & Prentice, D. A. (2002). Life task pursuit in social groups: Balancing self-exploration and social integration. *Self and Identity, 1*(2), 177–184.

Chu, B., & Kendall, P. (2004). Positive associations of child involvement and treatment outcome within a manual-based cognitive behavioral treatment with anxiety. *Journal of Consulting and Clinical Psychology, 72*, 821–829.

Corey, G. (2009). *Theory and practice of counseling and psychotherapy* (8th ed.). Brooks/Cole Cengage Learning.

Dispenza, F., Brown, C., & Chastain, T. E. (2016). Minority stress across the career-lifespan trajectory. *Journal of Career Development, 43*(2), 103–115. doi: 10.1177/0894845315580643

Durkheim, E., 1912 [1995]. *The Elementary Forms of Religious Life.* Oxford University Press.

Edwards, M., Adams, E. M., Waldo, M., Hadfield, O. D., & Biegel, G. M. (2014). Effects of a mindfulness group on Latino adolescent students: Examining levels of perceived stress, mindfulness, self-compassion, and psychological symptoms. *The Journal for Specialists in Group Work, 39*(2), 145–163. doi: 10.1080/01933922.2014.891683

Emdin, C. (2016). *For white folks who teach in the hood... and the rest of y'all too: Reality pedagogy and urban education.* Beacon Press.

Forsyth, D. R. (2010). *Group dynamics* (5th ed.). Belmont, CA: Wadsworth Cengage Learning.

Freire, P. (1970). *Pedagogy of the oppressed.* Continuum.

Freire, P. (2002). *Education for critical consciousness.* Continuum

Gabriel, S., Naidu, E., Paravati, E., Morrison, C. D., & Gainey, K. (2020). Creating the sacred from the profane: Collective effervescence and everyday activities. *The Journal of Positive Psychology, 15*(1), 129–154.

Gelso, C. J. (2009). The real relationship in a postmodern world: Theoretical and empirical explorations. *Psychotherapy Research, 19*, 253–264. doi:10.1080/10503300802389242

Ginter, E. J., Roysircar, G., & Gerstein, L. H. (2018). *Theories and applications of counseling and psychotherapy: Relevance across cultures and settings.* SAGE Publications.

Gladding, S. T. (2015). *Groups: A counseling specialty.* Pearson.

Glassman, U. (Ed.). (2008). *Group work: A humanistic and skills building approach* (Vol. *13*). SAGE.

Goldstein, S. E., Boxer, P., & Rudolph, E. (2015). Middle school transition stress: Links with academic performance, motivation, and school experiences. *Contemporary School Psychology, 19*(1), 21–29. doi: 10.1007/s40688-014-0044-4

Heerde, J. A., & Hemphill, S. A. (2018). Examination of associations between informal help seeking behavior, social support, and adolescent psychosocial outcomes: A meta-analysis. *Developmental Review, 47*, 44–62.

Karvelis, N. (2020). A Hip-Hop Pedagogy of Action: Embracing #BlackLivesMatter and the Teacher Strikes as Pedagogical Frameworks. In Adjapong, E. & Levy, I. (Ed). *#HipHopEd: A Compilation on Hip-Hop in Education Vol 2.* (pp. 1–5). Peter Lang Publishers.

Kelly, B. L., & Hunter, M. J. (2016). Exploring group dynamics in activity-based group work with young people experiencing homelessness. *Social Work with Groups*, 1–19.

Kottman, T., & Meany-Walen, K. (2016). *Partners in play: An Adlerian approach to play therapy.* John Wiley & Sons.

Levy, I., Emdin, C., & Adjapong, E. S. (2018). Hip-hop cypher in group work. *Social Work with Groups, 41*(1–2), 103–110. https://doi.org/10.1080/01609513.2016.1275265

Marino, R. C., Thornton, M. D., & Lange, T. (2015). Professional school counselors address grief and loss: A creative group counseling intervention. *VISTAS Online, Article, 66*, 1–12.

Pietkiewicz, I., & Smith, J. A. (2014). A practical guide to using interpretative phenomenological analysis in qualitative research psychology. *Czasopismo Psychologiczne – Psychological Journal, 20*, 7–14. doi:10.14691/CPPJ.20.1.7

Smith, J. A., Flowers, P., & Larkin, M. (2009). *Theory, method and research.* Sage Publications.

Snow, S., & D'Amico, M. (2010). The drum circle project: A qualitative study with at-risk youth in a school setting. *Canadian Journal of Music Therapy, 16*(1), 12–39.

Toseland, R. W., & Rivas, R. F. (2012). *An introduction to group work practice.* Allyn & Bacon.

Yalom, I. D., & Leszcz, M. (2005). *Theory and practice of group psychotherapy.* Taylor & Francis US.

7 HHSWT in a Comprehensive School Counseling Program

HHSWT in a Comprehensive School Counseling Program

When I began my work as a school counselor, like many other newly certified professionals, I was eager and willing to deploy my clinical skills. My initial goal, as explained consistently throughout this text, was to deploy culturally responsive approaches to counseling. However, likely as a function of my experience in my pre-service training program, I perceived my role as a school counselor to be quite similar to that of a mental health counselor who uses traditional long-term individual and group counseling. Understandably, my HHSWT pilot study focused directly on small-group counseling in an elective course as the vehicle for student's social/emotional development. While this is not inherently bad, I did not begin my work as a school counselor knowledgeable about the additional ways I could make HHSWT part of the school's educational programming to support student's holistic development.

As a testament to the beauty of hip-hop, and the brilliance of the students I worked with, we collectively and naturally learned to use HHSWT beyond small-group counseling. After hearing student's music, teachers began to see value in student's expression and inquired how they might incorporate hip-hop assignments in their classrooms to support academic outcomes and mitigate mental health concerns. The principal too noticed the importance of our group work and allowed for larger school initiatives (such as open mic nights and school-wide hip-hop showcases). Group sessions geared toward recording mixtapes garnered support from students' families and community members who functioned as consultants who offered beat-making workshops, DJing workshops, helped with live performance and assembled local media coverage to help advocate for the student's work. So, while I do not believe I was adequately prepared to be a school counselor when I entered the workforce, hip-hop, and my students, showed me how to become a school counselor who utilized interventions that transcended group and individual counseling to fill a bevy of important roles in the school ecosystem.

School Counselor Preparation and Development

The experiences I had entering the school counseling profession, with regard to my skill use and perceived abilities, are not novel. Many counselor education programs teach students to use basic counseling skills (Weger et al., 2010) which offer pre-service school counselors active listening behaviors that support dialogical conversations within schools (Ivey et al., 2013). Active listening skills can be used by school counselors when working with students, educators and other school stakeholders, or guardians to foster an empathetic relationship and encourage school-related outcomes such as learning, social and emotional development, and career exploration (Dollarhide et al., 2008). These same active listening and dialogical skills can be used as leadership strategies throughout the school environment, with the promise to create more cohesive and supportive school relationships between the various members of the school community (Bowers et al., 2018). However, within a great deal of school counseling master's programs (my alma mater included) students are not offered the chance to understand how to use counseling skills outside of traditional mental health contexts (long-term group or individual counseling). Further, active listening skills are irrelevant if school counselors are not taught to deploy them through a culturally competence lens, which explains why many school counselors begin their career without the cultural competence necessary to engage with Black and Brown youth (Dameron et al., 2020; Holcomb-McCoy, 2007). Couple this lack of learning to use culturally competent active listening skills, to address a variety of school counseling roles, with the reality that school counselors receive less professional development opportunities than almost any other school staff (Lowe et al., 2018), and my deer-in-headlights reaction to my first job makes sense. Lastly, unlike mental health counselors, school counselors do not receive steady and consistent supervision to support their future development of new skills to adequately tend to student's needs (Bledsoe et al., 2019).

In this book I have discussed how a pilot program encouraged further research on using HHSWT to: bolster rapport with students, design counseling offices, use mixtape making as action research in group work and foster group dynamics and therapeutic factors. Deploying HHSWT in any of these capacities requires that school counselors are able to utilize culturally competent active listening skills (in this case within the context of hip-hop) to engage in dialogical conversations with students. However, the bulk of the prior chapters zoom in on the school counselor's work in the context of small-group counseling and classroom instruction. This is done purposefully and is aligned with my personal growth as a school counselor using HHSWT. Through gleaning a deeper understanding of community-defined hip-hop cultural practices, my student's abilities and lived experiences, and hip-hop's propensity to generate systemic changes, came the knowledge regarding how HHSWT could pervade the school counselor's role. These skills and practices are imperative for school counselors who wish to use HHSWT but require specific and innovate professional development opportunities to learn. So, this final chapter explores the nuances of continuing to develop one's skills in order to both facilitate and maintain a comprehensive HHSWT program. To accomplish this goal, I will explore research from a mixed-methods study that sought to evaluate the effectiveness of a HHSWT professional development training series for practicing school counselors. Both the findings and implications of this study offer direction for the school counselor's facilitation and maintenance of HHSWT within a comprehensive school counseling program.

A HHSWT Professional Development Pilot

From February to May of 2019, I was consulted to provide a monthly 2-hour professional development workshop for 31 practicing school counselors in an Urban, Northeast School District in the United States. As part of my agreement with the school district, I was allowed to collect data for a mixed-methods study to evaluate the HHSWT professional development training series, also approved by my institution's internal review board. The goal of this study was to support school counselor's cultural competence and counseling skill self-efficacy development through the use of experiential hip-hop-based active listening activities. A series of training activities were developed to support counselors in hearing the affective and cognitive content communicated through hip-hop lyrics, as well as to design hip-hop-based group and classroom lesson plans. Data from pre- and post-training surveys, lyric-writing vignettes and post-training focus groups were collected and used in the analysis. This study was formally published in the *Journal of Counselor Preparation and Supervision* (Levy & Lemberger-Truelove, 2021) but in this chapter the curriculum is expanded upon and the results are re-considered to determine comprehensive HHSWT programming for school counselors.

Professional Development Curriculum

Identified throughout this text are a handful of HHSWT interventions (emotive lyric writing, collaboration as role-play, mixtapes as action research and the cypher) which cannot be used to support the construction of a strong therapeutic relationship, lead effective small-groups or build a larger comprehensive school counseling program, if school counselors are not able to hear the thoughts and feelings youth express through hip-hop lyrics and performance. The four-session professional development series curriculum was developed bearing this need in mind, aiming specifically to teach school counselors how to actively listen to the hip-hop students digest and create.

Session 1

The goal of the first professional development session was to provide practicing school counselors with knowledge of the theoretical constructions of HHSWT, as well as empirical data that spoke to its effectiveness. While the bulk of this first session was in a lecture format, I opened it (as I also would in sessions 2, 3 and 4) with an experiential cypher activity. The *cypher activity* is designed to enable participants to experience how it feels to share in a cypher space with their peers, including vulnerability, comradery and unity. In this activity, I formed a circle with all 31 counselors and began beat-boxing a steady rhythm. One-by-one, around the circle, each school counselor added a unique sound to the beat including clapping, stepping, audibly yelling a word or sound, tapping on a water bottle or any other organically created sound. By the end of the go-around, one large and complex beat was created, and anyone brave enough to freestyle rhymes was invited to do so. In this first session, I brought a colleague (a rapper) along with me who modeled this performance. After the cypher concluded, I facilitated a here-and-now reflection regarding what it was like to participate in the cypher. Some of these questions were pre-structured, like "What did it feel like to be in the cypher?" or "What did you notice about how others behaved in the cypher?", while I also relied on my facilitation skills to discuss any number of emergent thoughts or feelings. The remainder of the session was in lecture format and included interactive discussion using videos, student lyrics and data from the HHSWT studies explored within this book, offering a theoretical foundation for emotive lyric writing, collaboration as role-play, mixtapes as action research and the cypher as school counselors. This theoretical introduction to HHSWT, accompanied by an experiential cypher, aimed to communicate a robust picture about the potential of this work.

Session 2

The goal of the second training session was to teach and practice identifying affective and cognitive statements in hip-hop lyrics. The *cypher activity* was again open the group. Next, I lead a brief lecture that functioned as a "Rogerian refresher" where the core humanistic tenants of counseling were reviewed and provided a conceptual recap of basic micro skills (reflections, restatements, paraphrasing and summarizing). In a group, school counselors had a chance to practice actively listening for emotions and cognitions by listening to and reflecting on a pre-existing hip-hop song. For this *Hip-Hop Song Active Listening Activity*, participants were provided a highlighter, pen and printed lyrics to a song. As the song played over the speaker, participants were asked to highlight lyrics that spoke to specific feelings expressed by the artist. The song was then played a second time, and participants circled any lyrics that represented cognitions. A song titled "Neighbors" was used as an exemplar, where artist J. Cole details his experiences with racism living in an affluent, and mostly White, suburb. After the second listen, I facilitated a conversation around two structured questions: "What feelings did J. Cole express?" and "What is J. Cole thinking about in this song?", while I was also flexible and allowed a bevy of participants' reactions to be processed organically.

The practicing of hip-hop-based microskills continued through *Triadic Mock-Counseling Sessions*. As a means to model this exercise, a guest hip-hop artist and I engaged in a role-play demonstration. Pretending we were in an individual session, I functioned as a school counselor who listened to a student (played by a rapper colleague) read aloud lyrics he had created. As I listened to the lyrics, I noted a couple of different emotions and cognitions, and used reflections, restatements and paraphrasing statements about the content during a 5-minute dialogue. Then, participants were invited to separate into triads where they would rotate between the roles of a client, counselor and observer. The observer would keep time (5 minutes for the session) and utilize a rubric that rated the counselor's use of micro skills. The group was given a sheet with three snippets of hip-hop lyrics from popular rap songs. During each session the client would select one lyrical-snippet to share as their content for the session, as the counselor listened and responded with micro skills. When the session was completed, the client would offer feedback to the counselor, and observer would deliver their feedback, and the group roles would rotate. Session 2 closed out with a group reflection on how each activity went.

Session 3

In the third session, participants were to learn and practice the HHSWT tool of collaboration as role-play. The session opened with the *cypher activity* and was followed by a performance of an original song by a guest hip-hop artist. This time however, I engaged in a brief Q&A with the artist about their song, writing process and broke down their lyrics to illuminate the thoughts and feelings they processed in their lyric writing. Then, school counselors were told they would separate into five small-groups to co-create their own hip-hop song. Prior to beginning this breakout however, we decided on an agreed-upon emotional theme to explore. Using an online application (PollEverywhere), I had participants anonymously submit a single-word answer to the following question, "What is one word to describe how you are feeling at this point in the school year?". Submitted words were voted on, resulting in the school counselors deciding they would all write about feeling overwhelmed. Having selected a theme, counselors met in small-groups with the prompt of writing a 4-line chorus for their song as well as a 16-line collaborative verse. Groups were given a lyric writing worksheet which told them to discuss their emotional theme, to generate a list of both commonalities and individual differences, and then to use that list to construct their chorus and verse. The goal was for the group to learn about each other's experiences and attempt to lyrically play out a way through being overwhelmed. The session closed out with groups sharing their verses, including how the participants might utilize this exercise with their K-12 students.

Session 4

For the final session, participants learned to design lesson plans for group and classroom settings that would support students' use of mixtapes as action research. This session opened with a cypher, followed by a theoretical overview of the HHSWT critical cycle of mixtape making and a generic framework for tailoring mixtape making to meet the needs of their particular school and students. Brief data was shared to evince the effectiveness of mixtape making, and the group listened to and critiqued a student song about police brutality to understand how student research informed writing and disseminating information around an issue they deemed relevant to their lives. The main session activity was *Hip-Hop Lesson Plan Development* where school counselors broke into small-groups to design both a small-group and classroom instruction lesson. School counselors were told to use this one lesson as a launching point for a series of group and classroom sessions to complete a mixtape making process.

Relevant Instrument and Data Analysis

This mixed-methods study collected and analyzed participants' cultural competence, using the Cultural Competence Inventory-Revised (LaFromboise et al., 1991), and counseling skill self-efficacy, using the Counseling Self-Estimate Inventory (Larson et al., 1992). Two qualitative measures were used including a pre and post-training Hip-Hop Lyric Writing Vignette (where participants read a student verse for affective and cognitive content and completed short answer responses that asked them to write a reflection, paraphrasing statement and question in response to student lyrics), and a post-training focus group. Data analysis consisted of descriptive and inferential statistics, as well as an interpretive phenomenological analysis of participant focus groups. Specifically, the pre- and post-training survey data were analyzed using SPSS. The pre- and post-training hip-hop lyric writing vignettes were independently scored by me and a research assistant. Once consensus was reached, paired t-tests were used to compare pre- and post-training vignette scores. More information on these measures and analysis is available in the originally published study (Levy & Lemberger, in press).

Study Findings

Findings revealed that HHSWT, as a culturally appropriate professional development training series, can help school counselors refine their counseling skills. At pre-training participants reported very high measures of counseling skill self-efficacy (higher than the national mean), while simultaneously showing poor ability to utilize those same counseling skills on the hip-hop lyric writing vignettes (Levy & Lemberger-Truelove, 2021). This dissonance in reported and actual ability, with regard to counseling skill use, was noted at pre-training. At the post-course assessment, while the hip-hop lyric writing vignette score did not increase significantly, participant's post-training counseling skill self-efficacy decreased significantly. Data analysis suggested no significant changes in cross-cultural competence, with participants reporting high levels at both the pre-training and post-training assessments. These findings suggest that despite high self-reported cultural competence and counseling skill use, participants still struggled to deploy counseling skills (Levy & Lemberger-Truelove, 2021). The outcome of this training, therefore, appeared to be a humbling of school counselor's belief in their ability to perform counseling skills (as noted by the post-training decrease in self-efficacy to a level more reflective of their actual skills).

The qualitative data analysis produced three higher-order themes (each containing lower-order themes) that support the claim that school counselors became aware of how much more they needed to learn, as a result of participating in the HHSWT training series (Levy & Lemberger-Truelove, 2021). Participants reported that they *learned innovative practice* (including developing theoretical perspective, learning about practical tools and engaging in personal catharsis), *practiced humanistic counseling skills* (including working to understand youth culture, wanting to connect with students, using self in practice and developing new active listening skills) and *found new potential for student growth* (including finding hip-hop could help student's express thoughts and feelings easier, and address robust student outcomes; Levy & Lemberger-Truelove, 2021).

Implications for School Counselor's Development

In considering how participants could have reported very high counseling skill self-efficacy while they lacked actual counseling skill abilities, the Dunning- Kruger effect offers a potential rationale. The

Dunning-Kruger effect suggests that individuals who lack a skill will often hold a cognitive bias that enables them to overlook their own mistakes and erroneously assume sufficient abilities (Dunning, 2011). School counselors are in a tough place with regard to their counseling skill use and maintenance. As professionals who are asked to perform non-counseling tasks at alarming rates and have large caseloads that limit the amount of opportunities for direct counseling service (Mau et al., 2016), and who receive the least professional development compared to other educators (Lowe et al., 2018), it is not surprising that counseling skills might deteriorate overtime. Given the importance of counseling skills for the performance of school counseling roles, admitting to oneself that skills lack (at no fault of their own) is not easy. However, the qualitative data suggests that the samples of participants were potentially reconsidering their cultural awareness and knowledge, which typically occurs prior to developing culturally competent counseling skills (Worthington et al., 2007). The fact that the HHSWT allowed counselors to notice this skill deficit, and begin to work on it, is laudable (Levy & Lemberger-Truelove, 2021).

Suffice it to say, the first ever HHSWT training series did not produce school counselors who were ready to use HHSWT. However, the results support the need for continued professional development to support school counselors in recognizing culturally responsive skill deficits (Levy & Lemberger-Truelove, 2021) as a prerequisite to then learning to use new skills. Additionally, the HHSWT training series focused on counseling skill use as it pertains to emotion and cognitive content identification, lyric writing, collaboration as role-play, and the use of cyphers and mixtapes in group and classroom counseling. I believe it is first necessary for school counselors to realize their deficits, before we begin to teach new skills. I also believe that working on culturally responsive active listening offers school counselors the dialogical and relational skills to then deploy HHSWT in other capacities. Given this, future professional developments should consider the use of the pilot training's curriculum but then build on additional sessions exemplifying the potential of HHSWT to address additional parts of the school counselor's role.

HHSWT in a Comprehensive School Counseling Program

Each chapter in this book has detailed how small-group counseling, and in some instances classroom interventions, can be used to build authentic partnerships with youth that support their self-expression and identification of internal and external concerns. The HHSWT training series was built primarily to support those goals, to show how HHSWT tactics can be used toward social/emotional outcomes. Where the HHSWT training fell short was detailing how continued professional development would support school counselors in using HHSWT comprehensively to address the range of responsibilities. As is true with all of our work as counselors, gathering a deep understanding of students lived experiences and contexts (through the use of culturally sensitive basic counseling skills) serves as a guide to understanding how we can leverage all parts of schooling to support youth's holistic development. These responsibilities include collaborations with teachers, college and career readiness considerations, and leadership and advocacy work to collectively support students social/emotional, academic and career development. The final section of this chapter describes how HHSWT can permeate schooling.

Collaborations with Teachers Toward Academic Development

School counselors develop their small-group interventions for classroom settings to provide services to all students (ASCA, 2019; Henderson & Gysbers, 2006). School counselors collaborate and consult with teachers to help address social and emotional deterrents to academic development (Clark & Breman, 2009). Adjapong (2019) directed the Science Genius program in an urban school district, where students demonstrated science content knowledge through the writing and performing of hip-hop science songs. Adjapong's (2019) work validates the use of hip-hop approaches in science classrooms to support students' academic development – in this case science content knowledge. However, an earlier study on the science genius program found that asking students to write lyrics about academic content resulted in the unexpected emergence of student emotions (Emdin et al., 2016). The science genius program encourages teachers who are engaging in lyric writing about academic content, to consider having school counselors' push-in to offer social and emotional supports that aid in the attainment of academic outcomes. Additionally, school counselors might draw lessons from the HHWST training series to support teachers in practicing hip-hop-based active listening skills that can support students in feeling safe and validated when difficult emotions do emerge.

Addressing Student Emotions in Classrooms

It is undoubtedly necessary that teachers are able to tend to student's mental health needs on a daily basis, to alleviate emotional concerns that inhibit academic performance, and HHSWT can be quite beneficial toward this end. This is not to say that teachers are school or mental health counselors who help students uncover and process emotional stressors but is to suggest that daily emotional experiences germane to human development can be discussed in classrooms by teachers alone. Alongside my colleague Dr. Adjapong (a teacher educator), I co-developed a list of HHSWT-related classroom interventions that teachers can use to support student's mental health (Levy & Adjapong, 2020). As a school counselor educator and teacher educator, respectively, the development of a Hip-Hop Pedagogy and Mental Health model provides a practical example of school counselor and teacher collaboration. The Hip-Hop Pedagogy and Mental Health model details five classroom exercises, including: 1) Mental Health Journaling, 2) Graffiti Association, 3) Student Curated Mixtapes, 4) Group Cyphers and 5) Community Mental Health Awareness.

Mental Health Journaling draws from existing research emphasizing journaling as a platform for youth to authentically identify their own mental health concerns (Moses, 2019), and HHSWT's lyric writing as emotive journaling as a regular reflective practice (Levy, 2019). Mental Health Journaling was designed as an informal classroom strategy where, at the start of each class, students are offered time to lyrically reflect on the emotions they are bringing with them into the classroom, following a series of prompts, with the option to share if they choose. A concurrent daily practice is that of *Graffiti Association* which has students draw, paint, and/or collage pictures, words and/or phrases as a means to name and individually process emotional stress. Graffiti Association is rooted in research on art therapy which demonstrates drawing painting, coloring and collaging can help work through emotions (Walsh, 2019), develop emotional processing skills (Zimmer-Gembeck & Skinner, 2016), and decrease anxiety (Carlsey & Health, 2020). Using *Student Curated Mixtapes*, teachers work with their class to curate a collection of hip-hop instrumentals (songs without lyrics) around a specific emotional theme – for example, songs that remind students of positive moments in their lives. These student mixtapes can be played in the backdrop of each class, in alignment with what emotions students are bringing with them into the classroom. Having a range of mood playlists, co-created with students in moments where new emotions manifest, can help students cope with thoughts and feelings (Cook et al., 2019).

Group Cyphers encourage teachers to develop singular lessons around an emotional theme, ideally elicited from students, where students analyze and discuss an emotionally themed hip-hop music video or song before developing their own lyrics or artistic projects about that same emotional theme and share them out in a cypher. Traditional group cypher lessons adhere to the following structure: "1) a reflective do-now question about the emotional theme 2) a song or music video analysis, 3) a group discussion, 4) a small-group collaboration to create a product about the emotional theme and 5) a final share-out" (Adjapong & Levy, 2020, p. 19). Understanding that hip-hop is rooted in community advocacy, the tool of *Community Mental Health Awareness* draws from emotionally themed mixtape making (Levy et al., 2018) and Youth Participatory Action Research (Thorn et al., 2019) to support youth in research and disseminating projects about mental health issues to become change agents within their community. Each of these activities should be co-planned by a teacher and school counselor, where the school counselor plays an active role in either pushing into the classroom, or meeting with the teacher of ongoing support and consultation as curricular support as a catch-all for emotional issues that must be addressed outside of classrooms. There is a need to host additional professional development workshops with school counselors that help them facilitate active listening skills trainings, and lesson plan design workshops, to work with teachers toward social/emotional and academic outcomes.

College and Career Readiness

School counselors must also tend to student's career development through individual and group counseling, and classroom instruction. Career counseling scholars have called for the use of narrative counseling to support the development of resumes (Toporek & Flamer, 2009). Through story-telling activities, counselors can glean information regarding students' strengths, weaknesses, goals, skills and personality that not only inform the types of careers where a student might excel, but offer tangible information that can be placed on a resume. Returning to the use of HHSWT, counselors can have a student reflect on their career goals, past work experiences, strengths, skills (resume components) lyrically to then facilitate a conversation that informs the creation of physical resumes, or college application materials. Providing specific conceptual prompts to students like, write a song called "5-year plan", can help students discuss their short-term and long-term goals, which school counselors are responsible for helping students consider (ASCA, 2019). Drawing from other hip-hop elements, students could choose to also design a virtual vision board as a montage music video of images coinciding with the lyrics to their song.

Collaboration as role-play also has value in generating career-related outcomes. Rooted in Bandura's social learning theory (1997), role-play is used for the purpose of bolstering self-efficacy. Within the context of career work, cognitive processes like self-efficacy, self-knowledge and awareness, decision-making skills and self-talk are all deemed necessary for processing information and addressing career development tasks (Clemens & Milsom, 2008). For example, collaboration as role-play can be used to practice for interviews, fostering self-efficacy through constructing a song where students lyrically respond to mock-interview questions, or learn to talk about their strengths and showcase self-awareness. When faced with difficult college or career development decisions, lyric writing can be used as a pros-cons list activity where students write verses attempting to imagine themselves working a specific job or attending college on a specific campus. Knowing that college brings with it a slew of social and emotional challenges that can impact retention (Tello & Lonn, 2017), students might generate a list of potential social and emotional pitfalls in college and write individual songs to develop solutions to each concern. For example, Burt (2020) found a hip-hop small-group, where they both analyzed and wrote music, useful in supporting student's financial literacy. The transition to college is likely anxiety provoking and allowing students to reflect on this critical developmental moment lyrically can prove quite valuable (Thomson et al., 2002).

HHSWT in group, individual and classroom settings might open students' eyes to a variety of professions they were unaware of (Holland, 1997). Prior to HHSWT work, school counselors might use a personality assessment (such as Holland's career interest inventory) to generate a possible list of career options to reflect on. Researching and writing a mixtape about a variety of career options can allow each student to explore the fit of a potential job. However, the process of making a mixtape can reveal a handful of alternative career options that school counselors themselves might not even be aware of. For example, mixtape creation involves audio engineering and sound design, music production, graphic design for album art and concert fliers, social media marketing, photography and video editing, music video directing and script writing, clothing design and makeup, and choreography. Students might choose to design a podcast interview series with artists in the school, or a music blog to review new music from professional artists and students. If a school studio is constructed on campus, students can learn to manage artists and run a record-label. Mixtape making in particular calls for youth to engage in research and learning to present findings, which can be applicable in a variety of career settings. If intentional, bringing small-group, classroom or individual students through the creation of a multi-song mixtape, with a career interest assessment as a conversational baseline, can allow for the broadening of knowledge about, and exploration of, career opportunities. It should be noted that the goal of career work is not to turn youth into hip-hop artists but is to allow youth to pinpoint the ways hip-hop has naturally gifted them with the sensibilities (such as self-determination and self-awareness) necessary to exceed in a variety of professional arenas (Love, 2016), an area of career work in school counseling that certainty is deserving of more research. Professional developments with school counselors that specifically target CCR outcomes and aim to design small-group counseling and classroom instruction lessons are recommended.

HHSWT in Leadership and Advocacy

Beyond the use of HHSWT in individual, small-group and classroom settings to support social/emotional, academic and career development, school counselors must consider how to function as leaders in the building who advocate for school-wide approaches that serve all students. As leaders within the school building, school counselors must advocate for their role as professionals who can corral all educational stakeholders to positively influence student's development (ASCA, 2019). As advocates for social justice and cultural responsiveness who ensure the inclusion of youth voice in school counseling curriculum, school counselors must be thoughtful in how they critique and help alter school-wide policies and interventions to support all students (Holcomb-McCoy, 2007). These efforts are aligned with a theoretical premise of this text, to support school counselors in identifying oppressive school practices that minimize youth's ability to present themselves authentically (Emdin, 2016). In this final subsection, advisory councils, restorative justice, community partnerships and parent partnerships will be explored as larger schoolwide initiatives that infuse HHSWT practices.

Advisory Councils

ASCA (2012) defined Advisory Councils as "a representative group of stakeholders selected to review and advise on the implementation of the school counseling program" (p. 47). Organized by school counselors, advisory councils include administrators, parents, teachers, community members and students responsible for sharing schoolwide data and counseling goals with the school community. The school counselor can use the advisory council to get feedback on the functionality of their school counseling program, as well as input on the dissemination of school counseling curriculum (in classrooms, groups, individually and via school-wide events; ASCA, 2012). To facilitate and maintain HHSWT comprehensively, toward holistic development, school counselors should remember that contemporary hip-hop is constantly responding to and processing societal ills. Consequently, as advisory boards assess the needs of their student body, they must consider how to integrate current hip-hop music, news or other relevant media into their school counseling curriculum. To this end, having a student point-person on the board who is responsible for reporting on trends in hip-hop culture would be quite helpful. Sub-groups of teachers and counselors can meet, guided by the advisory council student, to create lessons for group counseling and classroom instruction and devise school-wide events. Advisory councils looking to measure the effectiveness (or lack thereof) of specific school policies in equitably supporting student development might arrange a small group of students to undergo a mixtape making process to research and report on inequities in school policy. Future professional development sessions for school counselors might explore how to form advisory councils specifically tailored to support the growth and maintenance of HHSWT.

Restorative Justice

Ample evidence exists detailing how the inequitable use of discipline practices marginalizes Black and Brown youth and constitutes one of many school policies that school counselors must interrogate (Holcomb-McCoy, 2007). The national center for educational statistic reports that Black boys are 2.4 times as likely to receive out-of-school suspensions compared to White boys, and Black girls are three times as likely to receive out-of-school suspensions compared to White girls (NCES, 2019). This data exists as a result of racist ideology that problematizes Black and Brown expression (Emdin, 2016; Love, 2019), validating what Hannon and Vereen (2016) would describe as reductionist view of Black youth. School counselors are responsible for disaggregating discipline data, to understand how it is unjustly used (Vincent et al., 2015), to inform the eradication of unjust polices in schools that negatively impact Black and Brown youth. Instead of penalizing student behavior researchers call for the use of restorative discipline practices that are both reparative and that promote an authentic understanding of student's lived experiences (Lustick, 2017; Payne & Welch, 2015).

HHSWT can be used by school deans, in collaboration with school counselors, to process a range of difficult emotions and oppressive school structures. For example, instead of relying on inequitable discipline practices that result in the over-suspension of Black and Brown youth, school counselors can partner with youth who have been incorrectly labeled as "misbehaving" on the construction of song and music videos that process external antecedents to internal feelings that result in behavior. This naturally cathartic process can allow youth to process emotional concerns that exist beneath behavior, rooted in a specific context and can support schools and students in co-designing policy that responds to a variety of forms of expression in a way that is preventative and developed, rather than punitive and harmful. Drawing from a Positive Behavioral Supports in Schools framework (Betters-Bubon et al., 2016), professional development can support the use of HHSWT informed Tier I, II and III interventions that support restorative justice practices. More research and hip-hop-centered restorative practices and trainings to help lead that work could be quite valuable for school counselors.

School–Family–Community Partnerships

School counselors possess a unique set of skills necessary to establish school–family–community partnerships, defined by Bryan et al. (2019) as "collaborative initiatives and relationships between school personnel, families, and community members who function as equal and mutual partners in the planning, coordinating, and implementing of programs and activities at home, at school, and in the community" (p. 266). These efforts can support students' social/emotional, college and career and academic outcomes (Holcomb-Mccoy & Bryan, 2010; Kaffenberger & O'Rorke-Trigiani, 2013; Trusty et al., 2008). Empowering parents and families that have been traditionally marginalized, through culturally appropriate means, to play an equal and active role in schooling, is paramount in this work (Bryan et al., 2019; Kim & Bryan, 2017). The reality that hip-hop is a multigenerational culture that, at a minimum, is relevant for students and their parents (Rawls & Petchauer, 2020), allows HHSWT to become a chief mechanism through which we engage parents and community members. Scholars note generational divides exist between elders and youth within the hip-hop community, with elders judging modern forms of hip-hop and being perceived by youth as out-of-touch and invalidating (Rawls & Petchauer, 2020). There is a need to bring youth, families and community together to find commonality and discover how hip-hop culture can be used to strengthen relationships and establish a collaborative schooling experience.

Anecdotally, I have experienced parents who expressed jealousy, wishing they had hip-hop programming during their secondary schooling years. Parents of students, or local community members, with an interest in hip-hop are actively available for consultation and collaboration with schools. For instance, offering parents or community members a small stipend to facilitate after-school programs that focus on beat-making, DJing, choreography, video editing, graphic or fashion design can assist students and family and community partnerships. Local community groups and organizations can become partners for youth's performance of their emotionally themed mixtapes, allowing for the disseminating of their research findings to the community in addition to the school. School counselors can create robust career fairs where local community members and parents who engage in work that is rooted in hip-hop aesthetics, creativity and/or sensibilities. Students can co-host open-mic nights at schools for students, parents and community members to attend. The value of HHSWT work is that it organically allows for the emergence of community and family partnerships, through actively listening to students' experiences and pushing them to consider how their families and communities can become involved in their work. Future trainings might involve tactics for assessing parents and community connection to hip-hop, and possible contributions to HHSWT.

Conclusion

A school counselor cannot develop, facilitate and maintain a HHSWT program without the proper knowledge and training to ensure that it pervades all components of the school ecosystem. Training of school counselors must begin with supporting their ability to use HHSWT as a culturally relevant approach for active listening in small-group and individual counseling. The use of dialogical skills supports the construction of a relationship with students built on a strong awareness of their lived experiences (affectively and cognitively) and social context. However, this deep level of knowledge is a prerequisite for considering how to create comprehensive school counseling curriculum that draws from small-group counseling, classroom instruction, collaborations with teachers, advisory councils, restorative justice and school–family–community partnerships to generate students social/emotional, academic and career development. Given the range of possibilities for the use of HHSWT in schooling, school counselors must receive ongoing professional develop that supports them in transcending group work to become active agents in the school community who not only offer a range of direct and indirect counseling services, but themselves offer valuable professional development to help other school professionals use HHSWT.

References

Adjapong, E. (2019). Towards a practice of emancipation in urban schools: A look at student experiences through the science genius battles program. *Journal of Ethnic and Cultural Studies, 6*(1), 15–27.

Adjapong, E.S., & Levy, I. (2020). Hip-hop can heal: Addressing mental health through hip-hop in the classroom. *The New Educator.* 10.1080/1547688X.2020.1849884

American School Counselor Association. (2019). *The ASCA national model: A framework for school counseling programs* (4th ed.) Author.

Bandura, A. (1997). The anatomy of stages of change. *American Journal of Health Promotion, 12*(1), 8–10. DOI: 10.4278/0890-1171-12.1.8

Betters-Bubon, J., Brunner, T., & Kansteiner, A. (2016). Success for all? The role of the school counselor in creating and sustaining culturally responsive positive behavior interventions and supports programs. *Professional Counselor, 6*(3), 263–277.

Bledsoe, K. G., Logan-McKibben, S., McKibben, W. B., & Cook, R. M. (2019). A content analysis of school counseling supervision. *Professional School Counseling, 22*(1), 1–8.

Bowers, H., Lemberger-Truelove, M. E., & Brigman, G. (2018). A social-emotional learning leadership framework for school counselors. *Professional School Counseling, 21*(1b). doi: 10.1177/2156759X18773004

Bryan, J., Griffin, D., Kim, J., Griffin, D. M., & Young, A. (2019). School counselor leadership in school-family-community partnerships: An equity-focused partnership process model for moving the field forward. In *The Wiley handbook on family, school, and community relationships in education*, 265–287.

Burt, I. (2020). I get money: A therapeutic financial literacy group for black teenagers. *The Journal for Specialists in Group Work, 45*(2), 165–181. https://doi.org/10.1080/01933922.2020.1740845

Carsley, D., & Heath, N. L. (2020). Effectiveness of mindfulness-based coloring for university students' test anxiety. *Journal of American College Health, 68*(5), 518–527. DOI: 10.1080/07448481.2019.1583239

Clark, M. A., & Breman, J. C. (2009). School counselor inclusion: A collaborative model to provide academic and social-emotional support in the classroom setting. *Journal of Counseling & Development, 87*(1), 6-11. DOI:10.1002/j.1556-6678.2009.tb00543.x

Clemens, E. V., & Milsom, A. S. (2008). Enlisted service members' transition into the civilian world of work: A cognitive information processing approach. *The Career Development Quarterly, 56*(3), 246–256.

Cook, N., Ingalls, M. M., & Trippett, D. (Eds.). (2019). *The Cambridge Companion to Music in Digital Culture.* Cambridge University Press.

Dameron, M. L., Camp, A., Friedmann, B., & Parikh-Foxx, S. (2020). Multicultural education and perceived multicultural competency of school counselors. *Journal of Multicultural Counseling and Development, 48*(3), 176–190.

Dollarhide, C. T., & Lemberger-Truelove, M. E. (Eds.). (2018). *Theories of school counseling for the 21st century.* Oxford University Press.

Dollarhide, C. T., Gibson, D., & Saginak, K. (2008). New counselors' leadership efforts in school counseling: Themes from a year-long qualitative study. *Professional School Counseling, 11*(4), 262–271.doi:10.1177/2156759X0801100407

Dunning, D. (2011). The Dunning-Kruger effect: On being ignorant of one's own ignorance. In J. Olson & M. P. Zanna (Eds.), *Advances in experimental social psychology* (Vol. *44*, pp. 247–296). Elsevier.

Emdin, C. (2016). *For White folks who teach in the hood... and the rest of y'all too: Reality pedagogy and urban education.* Beacon Press.

Emdin, C., Adjapong, E., & Levy, I. (2016). Hip-hop based interventions as pedagogy/therapy in STEM: A model from urban science education. *Journal for Multicultural Education, 10*(3), 307–321. doi:10.1108/JME-03-2016-0023

Hannon, M. D., & Vereen, L. G. (2016). Irreducibility of Black male clients: Considerations for culturally competent counseling. *The Journal of Humanistic Counseling, 55*(3), 234–245.

Henderson, P., & Gysbers, N. C. (2006). Providing administrative and counseling supervision for school counselors. *VISTAS: Compelling perspectives on counseling, 35,* 161-163. https://www.counseling.org/docs/default-source/vistas/providing-administrative-and-counseling-supervision-for-school-counselors. pdf?sfvrsn=8&sfvrsn=8

Holcomb-McCoy, C. (2007). *School counseling to close the achievement gap: A social justice framework for success.* Corwin Press.

Holcomb-McCoy, C., & Bryan, J. (2010). Advocacy and empowerment in parent consultation: Implications for theory and practice. *Journal of Counseling and Development, 88,* 259–268.

Holland, J. (1997). *Making vocational choices: A theory of vocational personalities and work environments* (3rd ed.) Odessa, FL: Psychological Assessment Resources.

Ivey, A. E., Ivey, M. B., & Zalaquett, C. P. (2013). *Intentional interviewing and counseling: Facilitating client development in a multicultural society.* Nelson Education.

Kaffenberger, C. J., & O'Rorke-Trigiani, J. (2013). Addressing student mental health needs by providing direct and indirect services and building alliances in the community. *Professional School Counseling, 16,* 323–332.

Kim, J., & Bryan, J. (2017). A first step to a conceptual framework of parent empowerment: Exploring relationships between parent empowerment and academic performance in a national sample. *Journal of Counseling and Development.* doi:10.1002/jcad.12129.

LaFromboise, T. D., Coleman, H. L., & Hernandez, A. (1991). Development and factor structure of the cross-cultural counseling inventory—revised. *Professional Psychology: Research and Practice, 22*(5), 380–388. doi:10.1037/0735-7028.22.5.380

Larson, L. M., Suzuki, L. A., Gillespie, K. N., Potenza, M. T., Bechtel, M. A., & Toulouse, A. L. (1992). Development and validation of the counseling self-estimate inventory. *Journal of Counseling Psychology, 39*(1), 105–120. doi:10.1037/0022-0167.39.1.105

Levy, I. (2019). Hip-hop and spoken word therapy in urban school counseling. *Professional School Counseling, 22*(1b), 2156759X19834436.

Levy, I., & Adjapong, E. S. (2020). Toward culturally competent school counseling environments: Hip-hop studio construction. *Professional Counselor, 10*(2), 266–284. Retrieved from https://files.eric.ed.gov/fulltext/EJ1259697.pdf

Levy, I., Cook, A. L., & Emdin, C. (2018). Remixing the school counselor's tool kit: Hip-hop spoken word therapy and YPAR. *Professional School Counseling, 22*(1), 1–18. https://doi.org/10.1177/2156759X18800285

Love, B. (2016). Complex personhood of hip hop and the sensibilities of the culture that fosters knowledge of self and self-determination. *Equity and Excellence in Education, 49*(4), 414–427. doi:10.1080/10665684.2016.1227223

Love, B. (2019). *We want to do more than survive: Abolitionist teaching and the pursuit of educational freedom.* Beacon Press.

Lowe, C., Gibson, D. M., & Carlson, R. G. (2018). Examining the relationship between school counselors' age, years of experience, school setting, and self-perceived transformational leadership skills. *Professional School Counseling, 21*(1b), 1–7. doi:10.1177/2156759X18773580

Lustick, H. (2017). "Restorative justice" or restoring order? Restorative school discipline practices in urban public schools. *Urban Education,* 0042085917741725.

Mau, W. C. J., Li, J., & Hoetmer, K. (2016). Transforming high school counseling: Counselors' roles, practices, and expectations for students' success. *Administrative Issues Journal: Connecting Education, Practice, and Research, 6*(2), 83–95. doi:10.5929/2016.6.2.5

Moses, C. (2019). Self-reflective Journaling: A Practice for Achieving Self-Understanding and Acceptance, Overcoming Creative Resistance, and Moving Toward Ideal Self. *Critical and Creative Thinking Capstones Collection. 375.* https://scholarworks.umb.edu/cct_capstone/375

National Center for Educational Statistics (2019). Status and trends in the education of racial and ethnic groups 2018 (NCES 2019-038). Retrieved from https://nces.ed.gov/pubs2019/2019038.pdf

Payne, A. A., & Welch, K. (2015). Restorative justice in schools: The influence of race on restorative discipline. *Youth & Society, 47*(4), 539–564.

Rawls, J. D., & Petchauer, E. (2020). "Be current, or you become the old man": Crossing the generational divide in hip-hop education. *Urban Education,* 0042085920914358.

Tello, A. M., & Lonn, M. R. (2017). The role of high school and college counselors in supporting the psychosocial and emotional needs of Latinx first-generation college Students. *Professional Counselor, 7*(4), 349–359.

Thomson, R., Bell, R., Holland, J., Henderson, S., McGrellis, S., & Sharpe, S. (2002). Critical moments: Choice, chance and opportunity in young people's narratives of transition. *Sociology, 36*(2), 335–354.

Toporek, R. L., & Flamer, C. (2009). The résumé's secret identity: A tool for narrative exploration in multicultural career counseling. *Journal of Employment Counseling, 46*(1), 4–17.

Trusty, J., Mellin, E., & Herbert, J. T. (2008). Closing achievement gaps: Roles and tasks of elementary school counselors. *The Elementary School Journal, 108*, 407–421. doi: 10.1086/589470.

Vincent, C. G., Sprague, J. R., Pavel, M., Tobin, T. J., & Gau, J. M. (2015). Effectiveness of schoolwide positive behavior interventions and supports in reducing racially inequitable disciplinary exclusion. In *Closing the school discipline gap: Equitable remedies for excessive exclusion*, 207–221.

Walsh, R. (2019). *Arts-based therapy group for urban youth. Special Topic: Social Work, Trauma, and the Arts Summer 2019 Course Anthology Bryn Mawr College Graduate School of Social Work and Social Research*, 128.

Weger Jr, H., Castle, G. R., & Emmett, M. C. (2010). Active listening in peer interviews: The influence of message paraphrasing on perceptions of listening skill. *The International Journal of Listening, 24*(1), 34–49. doi:10.1080/ 10904010903466311

Worthington, R. L., Soth-McNett, A. M., & Moreno, M. V. (2007). Multicultural counseling competencies research: A 20-year content analysis. *Journal of Counseling Psychology, 54*(4), 351–361. http://dx.doi.org/10.1037/0022-0167. 54.4.351

Zimmer-Gembeck, M. J., & Skinner, E. A. (2016). The development of coping: Implications for psychopathology and resilience. *Developmental psychopathology*, In D. Cicchetti (Ed.), (3rd ed., Vol. 4, pp. 485–544). Oxford: Wiley.

Conclusion
Hip-Hop and Spoken Word Therapy

This final chapter explores HHSWT as a holistic model for school counseling, containing a variety of elements detailed in each of the prior chapters. The culmination of the HHSWT model offers school counselors an approach to promote Black and Brown youth's voice and counter age-old oppressive educational practices. While this chapter functions mostly as a review of the HHSWT in its entirety, recommendations for the future of HHSWT are also considered. This text explored the development of Hip-Hop and Spoken Word Therapy (HHSWT) from its infancy. Beginning as a theoretical framework (Levy, 2012), HHSWT strategically coupled cognitive behavioral therapy, person-centered therapy, bibliotherapy and music therapy to offer hip-hop-based interventions that support student's exploration of difficult thoughts in feelings. Hip-hop cultural spaces were theorized as being culturally and socially acceptable environments for individuals to express vulnerabilities, making hip-hop lyric writing a potentially useful tool in the counseling process (Levy & Keum, 2014). HHSWT boasted the tools of lyric writing as a form of emotive journaling and collaborating as a role-play (where students work together on a song about a shared emotional theme). The original pilot study (Levy, 2019) empirically assessed the impart of a high school elective course that infused HHSWT and Reality Pedagogy, on student's coping skill development, emotional self-awareness and perceived stress. This pilot study, in addition to the follow-up studies explored within this book, operated from the humanistic belief (Rogers, 1957) that youth have the answers to their concerns, and that via the application of culturally competent counseling skills rooted in irreducibility (Hannon & Vereen, 2016), school counselors can support youth in pushing back against oppressive school structures that minimize their ability to self-actualize (Emdin, 2016).

Core Constructs

Analysis of the pilot study's findings set the groundwork for the further examination of what are now the core constructions of the HHSWT model. While the initial intent of the pilot program was to explore the impact lyric writing and collaborative song creation had on youth, a handful of other considerations emerged that warranted exploration, including 1) Can HHSWT support counselors in being authentic in session? 2) How do the co-creation of hip-hop studios support youth development? 3) What impact does mixtape creation have on the HHSWT process in group work? 4) How does the use of hip-hop cyphers as a sharing process support HHSWT? and 5) How do school counselors learn the skills needed to facilitate HHSWT in a comprehensive school counseling program? The exploration of each of these inquiries resulted in the framing of HHSWT as a culturally responsive approach to school counseling that contains the core constructs of: *Lyric Writing as Emotive journaling and collaboration as role-play, Establishing realness, Co-constructing school studios, Mixtape making, The hip-hop cypher* and *Training and comprehensive programming.*

Lyric Writing as Emotive Journaling and Collaboration as Role-play

The original core constructs of HHSWT were that of *lyric writing as emotive journaling* and *collaboration as role-play*. Both of these processes draw from having youth use lyric writing as a tool for the discussion, writing, recording and potential sharing of difficult emotional experiences in individual counseling and group work. Lyric writing as emotive journaling draws from cognitive behavioral and person-centered therapy (Beck, 1963; Rogers, 1957) tasking students with making daily journal entries, via lyric writing over a beat shared with them by their school counselor, which reflect on an emotional or behavioral topic they are working on in sessions. Collaboration as role-play pulls from the work of Bandura (1997) and has students work with their counselor, or a peer, to write songs that play out conversations around pressing emotional concerns or interpersonal challenges. Both lyric writing and collaboration in hip-hop culture broadly function as community-defined practices that youth engage in regularly and are thus included in the counseling process (Levy, 2019). The process of learning about the intricacies of community-defined practices, and using those to inform the development of HHSWT, spurred the development of the remaining core constructs.

Establishing Realness

Chapter 3 of this text substantiated the importance of the first additional construct to HHSWT – *establishing realness*, or authenticity in relationships with youth. Hip-hop school counselors believe that to sidestep historic and warranted feelings of mistrust of helping professionals from Black and Brown youth, they must become acutely aware of the ways in which youth define authenticity. For hip-hop culture, authenticity is a socially agreed upon construct used to combat the threat of assimilation (McLeod, 1999), which school counselors and youth are partnered in combating (Emdin, 2016). Authenticity in hip-hop is defined in six semantic dimensions which "draw upon [hip-hop] culture's most important symbols in ways that attempt to preserve its identity" (McLeod, 1999, p. 145). Specifically, McLeod (1999) defines the six dimensions of authenticity as: 1) Social-psychological, 2) Racial, 3) Political-economic, 4) Social-locational, 5) Gender-sexual and 6) Cultural. The practical application of HHSWT strategies of lyric writing, collaboration as role-play, hip-hop cyphers and mixtape making support the presence of these six authenticity dimensions in sessions (Levy, 2020). However, the deployment of HHSWT strategies requires school counselors to develop and sustain cultural humility as to not wrongfully appropriate hip-hop culture and further oppressive the youth they serve. *Establishing realness* as a core HHSWT construct offers practical assistance to school counselors in the self-exploration needed to deploy HHSWT and build strong relationships.

Co-Constructing School Studios

Moving beyond the relational dynamics, Chapter 4 considered the impact of a hip-hop-inspired counseling environment. Through the re-analysis of data from a prior research study (Levy & Adjapong, 2020), *Co-constructing school studios* as a core construct in the HHSWT group-work process was illuminated. Believing in the ability of youth to determine the right environment for their own development, and to establish a physical place within school buildings where they can authentically express themselves (Emdin, 2016), the co-construction of hip-hop recording studios are efficacious. Research indicates that hip-hop studios are culturally specific spaces or places where individuals find meaning, interact with one another and feel legitimized as they personally transform and develop (Harkness, 2014). School counselors who co-construct recording studios as counseling offices with their students can help establish culturally sound school spaces for identifying areas of growth, maintaining authenticity and feeling confident. School studios are also noted to have a large impact on school culture in that they promote student advocacy and leadership, cohesion and continuous self-work. Studio co-construction is not about generating the funding or resources for state-of-the-art studios, but instead trusting youth to organically design a place they feel comfortable within.

Mixtape Making

Inside of studios, and during HHSWT work, students collaborate on making emotionally themed mixtapes, often as a form of action research.

Mixtape making also holds value as a community-defined hip-hop cultural practice used as a means to uplift voices and share untold stories, particularly in ways that speak back against oppressive structures (Ball, 2011). Chapter 5 covered the intricacies of HHSWT core construct, *mixtape making*, as a group work process. Mixtape making has theoretical grounding in action research, humanism and honoring youth voice (Levy et al., 2018a). Practically mixtape making is a mailable guide to group work in that it can be facilitated with a number of structures and leadership styles that are empirically validated and positively impact youth's well-being (Levy & Travis, 2020). An analysis of student lyrics from two separate mixtapes found mixtape making is a medium through which students can interrogate, and emotionally process, any themes they deem relevant to their lives, spurring the opportunity for sharing thoughts, feelings and research with their school community.

The Hip-Hop Cypher

As a hip-hop cultural process, *hip-hop cyphers* were originally theorized as group environments that contained the dynamics and therapeutic factors necessary for healing (Levy et al., 2018b). Prior to assessing the impact cyphers have on youth, however, Chapter 5 evaluated this theoretical supposition by studying the value that hip-hop cyphers have for the hip-hop community. A series of qualitative interviews with rappers indicated that, within hip-hop cyphers, participants experienced valuable communication and interaction (including *interpersonal communication and relationship building, developing cohesion, empowerment by competition, conflict and tension resolution and spiritual connection*), intrapersonal development (including *developing comfort expressing, catharsis and personal growth*) and navigating norms and roles (including *adhering to unspoken rules and noticing roles*). Findings confirm that hip-hop cyphers contain many of the group dynamics and therapeutic factors traditional literature deems necessary for successful group development. Implications for the use of cyphers in schools with youth were also explored, naming the *hip-hop cypher* a core construct of HHSWT.

Training and Comprehensive Programming

A final core construct of HHSWT pertains to the professional development necessary to maintain skills for facilitating comprehensive school counseling programming, named *training and comprehensive programming*. While the aforementioned constructs of HHSWT are situated within small-group counseling mainly, comprehensive programming refers to the school counselor's ability to infuse HHSWT into all aspects of their roles within the school building. To begin HHSWT work, school counselors must undergo training in the use of hip-hop-based active listening skills – to ensure they are able to deploy dialogical and relational counseling skills with youth who identify as hip-hop. As is true with all of the school counselor's work, gathering a deep understanding of students' lived experiences and contexts (through the use of culturally sensitive counseling skills) serves as a guide to understanding how we can leverage all parts of schooling to support youth's holistic development. Comprehensive programming guides school counselors in using HHSWT to promote student's social/emotional, academic and career development though collaborations with teachers, college and career readiness as well as leadership and advocacy.

Future Directions for HHSWT

Preparing to write this monograph, at first, felt like the culminating event at the end of a long line of research. However, as I have discovered in all of my work with HHSWT – I am left with more questions than answers. A noted limitation to many of the HHSWT research studies reviewed in this text is the smallness of the sample sizes. However difficult it may be to engage in an analysis of a HHSWT construct with a large sample sizes in schools, it remains necessary.

Additionally, this project presents a slew of alternative lines of inquiry deserving of research. For example, a large dissemination of a HHSWT intervention requires a legion of school counselors who have been adequately training. Training might happen in two ways. Following the small training study that I conducted (Levy & Lemberger-Truelove, 2021), partnerships with district offices for ongoing professional development sessions might prove fruitful. In these trainings, the curriculum and subsequent assessments of the counselor's growth must incorporate the use of HHSWT in comprehensive programming. Another option is developing school-counselors-in-training to use HHSWT during their graduate coursework. Graduate students could receive training from a school counselor educator, who then supervises their direct work during their internship experiences. There is potential for HHSWT training to generate school counselors' cultural and social justice competencies, and racial identity development, in support of a more equitable school system that validates and assists in youth's authentic development.

Regardless, training of school counselors in any capacity would support a multi-school dissemination study. In such study, it is recommended that all core constructs be explored. The use of hip-hop cyphers in group counseling with youth directly requires immediate empirical support. While certainly a complicated study that could take many forms, measuring the therapeutic alliance while using HHSWT is fascinating. Empirically assessing the use of the Hip-Hop Pedagogy and Mental Health model (Adjapong & Levy, 2020) could greatly support the use of HHSWT informed practices in classrooms, in addition to the collaborative efforts of school counselors and teachers. Documenting and evaluating the work of youth-led advisory councils that infuse HHSWT toward equitable school policy is deserving of additional research as a school-wide intervention. Lastly, career development, as informed by HHSWT, holds promise but has limited conceptual and empirical support. Scholars are highly encouraged to explore this area, building off the hip-hop sensibility work of Love (2016). In order to support schools in the direct dissemination of HHSWT, the provision of a practical guide or workbook for school counselors is necessary. Whatever direction this research takes in the field of school counseling, I urge us to remember to constantly trust Black and Brown youth as the bearers of all of the knowledge needed to actualize their full potential and to be unrelenting in our fight to support their authenticity and autonomy.

References

Adjapong, E.S., & Levy, I. (2020). Hip-hop can heal: Addressing mental health through hip-hop in the classroom. *The New Educator*. 10.1080/1547688X.2020.1849884

Bandura, A. (1997). The anatomy of stages of change. *American Journal of Health Promotion: AJHP, 12*(1), 8–10.

Beck, A. T. (1963). Thinking and depression: I. Idiosyncratic content and cognitive distortions. *Archives of General Psychiatry, 9*(4), 324–333. doi:10.1001/archpsyc.1963.01720160014002

Emdin, C. (2016). *For white folks who teach in the hood... and the rest of y'all too: Reality pedagogy and urban education.* Beacon Press.

Hannon, M. D., & Vereen, L. G. (2016, October 1). Irreducibility of black male clients: Considerations for culturally competent counseling. *Journal of Humanistic Counseling.* doi: 10.1002/johc.12036

Harkness, G. (2014). Get on the mic: Recording studios as symbolic spaces in rap music: Get on the mic. *Journal of Popular Music Studies, 26*(1), 82–100. doi: 10.1111/jpms.12061

Levy, I. (2012). Hip hop and spoken word therapy with urban youth. *Journal of Poetry Therapy, 25*(4), 219–224. doi: 10.1080/08893675.2012.736182

Levy, I. (2019). Hip-hop and spoken word therapy in urban school counseling. *Professional School Counseling, 22*(1b), 2156759X1983443. doi: 10.1177/2156759X19834436

Levy, I. (2020). "Real recognize real": Hip-hop spoken word therapy and humanistic practice. *The Journal of Humanistic Counseling, 59*(1), 38–53. doi: 10.1002/johc.12128

Levy, I. & Adjapong, E. S. (2020). Toward culturally competent school counseling environments: Hip-hop studio construction. *The Professional Counselor, 10*(2), 19.

Levy, I., Cook, A. L., & Emdin, C. (2018a). Remixing the school counselor's tool kit: Hip-hop spoken word therapy and YPAR. *Professional School Counseling, 22*(1), 2156759X18800285. doi: 10.1177/2156759X18800285

Levy, I., Emdin, C., & Adjapong, E. S. (2018b). Hip-hop cypher in group work. *Social Work with Groups, 41*(1–2), 103–110. doi: 10.1080/01609513.2016.1275265

Levy, I., & Keum, B. T. (2014). Hip-hop emotional exploration in men. *Journal of Poetry Therapy, 27*(4), 217–223. doi: 10.1080/08893675.2014.949528

Levy, I., & Lemberger-Truelove, M. E. (2021). Supporting Practicing School Counselor's Skill Development: A Hip Hop and Spoken Word Professional Development Intervention. *The Journal of Counselor Preparation and Supervision* 14(1). Retrieved from https://repository.wcsu.edu/jcps/vol14/iss1/7.

Levy, I., & Travis, R. (2020). The critical cycle of mixtape creation: Reducing stress via three different group counseling styles. *Journal for Specialists in Group Work, 45*(4), 307–330. doi: 10.1080/01933922.2020.1826614

Love, B. (2016). Complex personhood of hip hop and the sensibilities of the culture that fosters knowledge of self and self-determination. *Equity and Excellence in Education, 49*(4), 414–427. doi: 10.1080/10665684.2016.1227223

McLeod, K. (1999). Authenticity within hip-hop and other cultures threatened with assimilation. *Journal of Communication, 49*(4), 134–150. doi: 10.1111/j.1460-2466.1999.tb02821.x

Rogers, C. R. (1957). The necessary and sufficient conditions of therapeutic personality change. *Journal of Counseling Psychology, 21*(2), 9.

Index

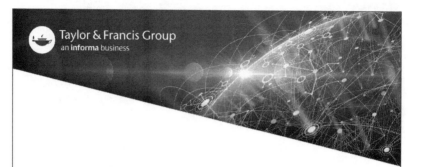